I0060058

Coaching
For Success
A Guide to
The Art of
Life Coaching

DR. BILL GRAYBILL

Copyright © 2015 by Bill Graybill
www.billgraybill.com

All rights reserved. No part of this book may be reproduced
in any form or by any electronic or mechanical means,
including information storage and retrieval systems—except
in the case of brief quotations embodied in critical articles or
reviews—without permission in writing from its publisher or
authorization by the author.

First Edition Printed, 2015

Published by:
Peace Mentors
34510 Mountain View Pl NE
Albany, OR 97322

Unless otherwise marked, Scripture quotations are from the
HOLY BIBLE, NEW INTERNATIONAL VERSION®.
NIV®. Copyright© 1973, 1978, 1984 by International Bible
Society. Used by permission of Zondervan Publishing House.
All rights reserved.

This publication is designed to provide accurate and
authoritative information in regards to the subject matter
covered. It is sold with the understanding that the publisher
or author is not engaged in rendering legal, counseling or
other professional service. If legal advice or other expert
assistance is required, the services of a competent, licensed
professional person should be sought.

ISBN: 978-0-9844195-6-2

DEDICATION

This book is dedicated to my wife, Dorothy.

For over forty years you believed in me and cheered me on, during easy time and hard times. Thank you for being a part of this amazing journey with God.

CONTENTS

Dr. Bill Graybill

INTRODUCTION

"Everybody's a coach in some aspect of life, and that means you. Regardless of whether you have an official title, there are people out there who need your help."

—Ken Blanchard

You are a coach in someone's life. They are counting on you to be what they need. Someone who will come along side and help, not by telling them what to do, but by exploring the options with them. They will make the necessary decisions. It is your job to help them investigate the possibilities and give them the freedom and power to choose what's best for them.

This book is intended to give an overview of life coaching. Together, we will explore some of the skills necessary, even practicing those skills and experiencing the joy of watching the triumph of new insights in those with whom you are working.

Coaching for Success; A Guide to the Art of Life Coaching is a primer, not meant to be comprehensive or exhaustive. Once you have a taste, you'll be able to go on to other resources to develop and refine your coaching skills. You may be on your first leg in a long and rewarding journey called life coaching.

The greatest bit of advice I can give you is simple. Enjoy the journey.

1

WHAT'S COACHING ALL ABOUT

Coaching is an amazing and effective tool to overcome obstacles and find success. This book being written is a result of my being coached. Actually, it was a group of beginners who coached me!

I was teaching a coaching 101 class at a local seminary; all the students were new to coaching. For a skills practice, I had the students coach me as a class. I was stuck and could not see how I was going to write this book before the deadline. Overwhelmed and discouraged, I started to look for Plan B.

The class started out with, "What would you like to take away from this coaching session?"

Bill: "I have a book to write and don't see how I can do it before the deadline."

Class: "What would be helpful?"

Bill: "A plan."

They coached me for about 20 minutes with their new skills. I ended the practice with a two-part plan that propelled me over the hurdle of feeling paralyzed. The students had a new sense of the power of coaching and the satisfaction of helping someone be successful.

WHAT IS COACHING?

In dictionaries, usually the first definition is about a horse-drawn carriage. They will go on to describe other types of transportation. Secondly, they will discuss the idea of an instructor or trainer, usually focusing on athletics.

The origin of the word comes from a Hungarian town called Kocs. It was here that the first carriage was made and named. The term coaching was first applied to an instructor around 1830 at Oxford University. It was slang for a tutor who "carries" a student through an exam. In 1861 it was first applied to sports in the area of boat racing.

Wikipedia defines coaching as "training or development in which a person called a 'coach' supports a learner in achieving a specific personal or professional goal." The person being coached is often called a coachee or pbc (person being coached).

Timothy Gallwey, author of *The Inner Game of Tennis* and *The Inner Game of Work*, offers an excellent sense of what coaching is: "Coaching is unlocking a person's potential to maximize their own performance. It is helping them to learn rather than teaching them."

The International Coach Federation, the largest and most well-known coaching organization, defines coaching as "an ongoing professional relationship that helps people produce extraordinary results in their lives, careers, businesses, or organizations. Through the process of coaching, clients deepen their learning, improve their performance and enhance their quality of life."

Gary Collins, well known in Christian counseling circles, defines coaching as the "art and practice of guiding a person or group from where they are toward the greater competence and fulfillment that they desire."[1]

As you can see, coaching is all about going forward and seeing positive results. This process is not new. Both Aristotle and Socrates used this approach in helping people learn and move forward. The principles and practices of coaching are over two thousand years old, and in the last 30 years have gained renewed interest and popularity.

Sir John Whitmore highlights the key issue when he observes, "the objective of improving performance is paramount, but how it is best achieved is what is in question."[2]

IT IS NOT...

Coaching is not "telling." I've been in conversations about coaching where one person will look at their friend and say, "You'd make a good coach. You really give good advice." Giving good advice, or even great advice, is not the point of coaching. Most people already know what to do, they simply need help moving forward.

Coaching is not about authority; it is a partnership with equal status. A coach is not the boss assigning work, but a teammate who is offering to walk alongside and offer the skills needed to bring forward movement.

---

[1] Gary Collins, Christian Coaching (Colorado Springs: NavPress, 2001), 16.

[2] John Whitmore, Coaching for Performance, third edition (London: Nicholas Brealey, 2002), 7.

Coaching is not about being the expert. In reality, a good coach can be highly effective in areas they know nothing about. Some leaders and pastors desire coaches who are not experts in the client's field but rather are exceptionally skilled coaches who are experts in moving people forward.

Coaching is not fixing people or situations. When someone comes to you for help, most people's natural tendency is to fix the problem. Sometimes that means fixing the person by telling them what they need to do or how they need to act. Other times it is about fixing the problem by giving advice or intervening with instructions.

IT IS …

Coaching is about drawing out what is already inside the coachee. There is a basic belief in coaching that the best answers for the coachees are found within, by the coachees themselves.

Coaching offers new awareness and discovery made by the coachee. When you discover something for yourself it has deeper impact than being told the same information. Coaching offers the opportunity for self-discovery.

Coaching hands new ideas back to the coachee. The magic of coaching is found by the coachee making all the discoveries and decisions. When a new idea or thought is noticed, it is the coachee who gets to make any observations and decisions needed.

Coaching enables the coachee to create, own and execute the steps forward. As the coachee discovers new options and finds new alternatives, he or she is ready to move forward. In the past, a mentor might explain what the next steps are. In coaching, the coachee gets to design the action plan and make the necessary commitments to carry it out. Coaching creates a higher probability of follow-through, because the coachee has a greater investment in the plan.

Coaching is focused on the future, while counseling is focused on the past, coaching turns towards the future. This requires a healthy coachee who is not stuck in the past or hung up on past events and hurts. A basic assumption in coaching is that the coachee is ready to embrace a new future.

In the next chapter we will look at why life coaching has become so popular.

I have included additional resources to help you understand and excel at coaching. To download these resources go to billgraybill.com/IntroCoachingResources

Dr. Bill Graybill

2

WHY IS EVERYONE TALKING

ABOUT IT

I sat in my office listening to a couple tell me why their marriage was in trouble. According to the wife, all he was interested in was going to the sand dunes with the guys and riding the dune buggy. His complaint was that she was always over at her mom's house. When they were home together all she could do was find fault with everything he did. He felt he could never please her.

What made this scene sad was that no matter what I told them to do, they always came back with the same story. Had they done what I suggested? No. Had they practiced the skills I taught them? No. What had they done? Nothing. But here they were, wanting help, but not willing to do what I suggested.

Scenes like this are common in pastors' offices all around the world. Why? Because people do not do what they are told, but, what they create themselves. When you are told that you need to do something, and there is no internal buy-in, it just won't happen.

I quit pastoral counseling over ten years before leaving the lead pastor role. I found it discouraging and ineffective. Visit after visit, people would come into my office, dump their feelings in the middle of the room, tell me they wanted to change, and ask what they should do. Then they would go out and do none of the things I suggested. When I found coaching, I found a tool with greater success than I ever experienced in counseling.

WHY IS COACHING BECOMING SO POPULAR?

According to the The International Coach Federation (ICF), Coaching is becoming popular for several reasons.

Many people are tired of doing what they "should" do and are ready to do something special and meaningful for the rest of their lives. The problem is, many can't see it, or if they can, they can't see a way to re-orient their life around it. A coach can help them do both.

People are realizing how simple it can be to accomplish something that several years ago might have felt out of reach, or like a pipe dream. A coach isn't a miracle worker, but a coach does have a large tool kit to help your "Big Idea" become a reality.

Spirituality. One of the emerging trends cited by the World Future Society is our growing sense of spirituality. Many coaches are spiritually based and coach from a place of values and world view—even the ones who coach Fortune 500 Companies. A coach helps clients tune in better to themselves and others.

The arena of business coaching is also very popular. This is true for Fortune 500 companies or entrepreneurs who have a one-person business. I have worked with my present business coach for over three years; I receive great value every time I am coached.

WHY DO ORGANIZATIONS VALUE COACHING?

The quickening pace of change requires organizational leaders to develop quickly while still remaining in their current position. There is no time to go back to school. Coaching offers an individualized development option without removing leaders from their work.

Great talent is in high demand across the business world. As the need to find and retain quality employees intensifies, many organizations view coaching as a way to compete in the marketplace to attract and retain employees with the needed expertise.

WHEN IS COACHING THE RIGHT ANSWER?

Coaching is a tool, not the answer to every problem or situation. As a new coach, I thought coaching was the only tool I needed. It is like the old saying, "If you have a hammer, everything looks like a nail."

Sometimes coaching is the best answer, other times perhaps counseling or mentoring is a better answer. It is important to note the differences between these tools and to know when to use them. The following chart explains the differences between the four main tools.

Comparing Different Helping Processes				
	Coaching	Mentoring	Therapy	Consulting
Who is the expert	The client	The mentor	The therapist	The consultant
Assumption about the client	Healthy	Lacks experience	Has problems	Needs an expert
Purpose of questions	To promote discovery	Questions come from student	To diagnose	To gather data
Why you are listening for	To know the next question	To find gaps in experience	To understand the past	To form solutions
What is your role	A co-equal partner	To show and tell	To give solutions	To create a plan of action
Results	Client creates plan and actions	Be like me, do what I did	Under-standing and acceptance	Proposed solutions delivered

There are some key assumptions when it comes to coaching. In my opinion, one of the main assumptions is that the coachee is healthy, both emotionally and spiritually. If the coachee is not healthy, then coaching will not be the best tool. A key decision to seeing success is in picking the right process for the person seeking your help.

I do conflict resolution coaching; therefore, I must make sure my clients are ready for coaching and not in need of counseling. If they are stuck in the past and are paralyzed, then it is time to refer them to someone who can help them deal with the past hurts and become healthy, ready to move into the future.

Here is a list of common benefits you can expect from coaching:
- Improved sense of direction and focus.
- Increased knowledge of self and self-awareness.
- Improved ability to relate to and understand others.
- Increased motivation.
- Improved personal effectiveness.
- Increased resourcefulness.
- Increased ability to handle change.
- Increased creativity.

Martin Seligman, the founder and pioneer of positive psychology, says life coaching revolves around the essential question: Do you want to be pulled by your future or driven by your past? This is the key question when it comes to deciding between a coach and a counselor.

In the next chapter we will look at the where and how of coaching.

I have included additional resources to help you understand and excel at coaching. To download these resources go to billgraybill.com/IntroCoachingResources

Dr. Bill Graybill

3

THE WHERE AND HOW

I found myself sitting in the airport after a long three days of coach training. It was my first class in this new adventure. I was tired, but in awe of what I had experienced over the preceding days, and wondering how I was going to use this new tool in my ministry.

Sitting next to me was a business woman on her way home to San Francisco, tired and ready to call it a day. We struck up a conversation (which is rare for me when I travel as I like to play the part of an introvert). Soon we were discussing her foster daughter and how to handle a tough set of circumstances.

I had two totally different approaches warring in my mind. Do I go with the pastor approach and give advice, or will it be the coach who works to bring out her best solution? The coach won, and for the next 30 minutes I had a significant exchange that opened my eyes to the powerful dynamics of coaching. She boarded the flight with a specific plan, created within her own framework and skills. The word "coaching" was never used in our conversation.

INFORMAL COACHING

Informal coaching is generally the most common type of coaching you will do. There will be many opportunities to help others with a few powerful questions. Whether it is at work or a social occasion, you will see many openings to simply help someone take a step forward by using your coaching skills.

Be warned, however, not everyone wants to be coached. Don't hop into your coaching voice or persona. Be curious and reflect back to them what you hear, and drop in a question now and then. You will part having given them a gift.

When I am in informal settings and the occasion presents itself to coach the other person, I always ask permission. I'll say something like, "Mind if I ask a few questions?" People who know me well know that they are about to receive a free coaching session. Sometimes I get a, "No," and that is okay also.

Informal coaching can happen anywhere, any time and in any place. It is simply using the practice of coaching skills as a means of relating to, supporting and serving another person. Be ready. Be sensitive. Be humble. You will be surprised by what comes your way.

FORMAL COACHING

You may do formal coaching if you choose to create the space and opportunities that will open the door. Formal coaching is usually done with acknowledging what is about to happen, is formal, and has certain trappings that go with it.

You will have some sort of written agreement as to what you are doing and how it will be done. This will include the understanding that coaching is not therapy or counseling. It might also include the duration of your coaching and if there is a cost.

At the beginning of your coaching conversation, you will set up the parameters of what you hope to accomplish during the session and what will be a positive outcome. This may already have been determined by a supervisor or a previous conversation. It may be long-term or short-term in duration. Formal coaching generally includes the component of accountability. This accountability can take many shapes and is best when designed by the coachee.

LIVE AND IN-PERSON COACHING

In the classes I have taught to beginning coaches, we talk about live and in-person coaching. The majority want to coach in person, believing it is more effective and feels better. I can understand this because I like to interact with people in person. I presently do a mix of in-person and phone coaching. Personally, I like phone coaching better. I'll tell you why in the next section.

With 70-90 percent of communication non-verbal, in-person coaching has a lot of opportunity to observe emotions, reactions, body and facial changes. Observation is a powerful coaching skill. Another advantage of in-person coaching is the ability to interact with on-the-spot drawings and diagrams. I am always grabbing a napkin at Starbucks and drawing a diagram that illustrates a concept. Please note, while I coach at coffee houses, most of it is done in private settings.

In-person coaching allows for the giving and receiving of unspoken encouragement and affirmation. Throw in the enjoyment of being with people and in-person coaching becomes attractive.

PHONE COACHING

Given the choice, I will coach by phone. I believe it is more effective and a better value for the coachee.

Remember how up to 90% of information taken in during a face-to-face conversation is visual? That should make face-to-face coaching 10 times more effective than telephone coaching, but it doesn't. Why? Because nearly all of that visual information is unconscious, meaning the coach isn't even aware of it.

A well-trained coach will be very aware of what is happening with the coachee just by listening. I know of one coach who wears a blindfold while coaching to enhance his listening skills. I find that I get too much information visually and it distracts from what I am hearing or not hearing.

Another reason for coaching by phone is the convenience factor: no driving hassle, no parking, and less time spent since there's no commute involved. I take a 15-minute break between clients to gather my thoughts and transition to a new coachee. This would be impossible if I was doing the traveling.

Then there's the fact that coaching by phone offers a bit more anonymity, and that may encourage you to open up more and to feel less compromised after a session. You can talk from the comfort of your own home, in an environment that feels safe and nourishing.

INDIVIDUAL COACHING VS GROUP COACHING

There is one last area to look at in this chapter. Group coaching is becoming very popular, and has many benefits. This type of coaching opens up a whole new world. Let's quickly look at the differences. We will spend an entire chapter on the topic of group coaching and mastermind groups. I have provided the following chart of characteristics.

Characteristics of Individual Coaching	Characteristics of Group Coaching
Coachee-driven agenda	Project- or program-driven agenda
Greater flexibility	Ability to hear other's questions and input
Greater knowledge of the coachee	Larger pool of resources and creativity
Private	Better format for team building
Higher cost per person	Lower cost per person

Next we will explore the coaching model. You will discover how to formulate the coaching conversation, what is included, and in what order. You will also learn the steps necessary to become a good coach.

Dr. Bill Graybill

4

TEACH ME TO COACH

Susan looked at me with a perplexed look on her face that cried out for help. She wasn't the only one who had that look. Susan was doing her first practice coaching exercise with a real live coachee and she felt stuck.

Whenever I teach a coaching 101 class, most of the students have the same look as Susan. New to coaching and without a coaching track to run on, they struggle to know what to do or say next. While very common, it evokes a sense of panic. To overcome this struggle we turn to a coaching model that will give structure and direction to the coaching process.

HOW DOES COACHING WORK?
For coaching to be effective the coach and the coachee are active collaborators. This relationship is an alliance between two equals for the purpose of meeting the coachee's needs.

Forming this relationship is built around four foundational pillars.[3]

- The coachee is naturally creative, resourceful, and whole.
- The agenda is designed by the coachee.
- The coach moves with the coachee.
- Coaching addresses the coachee's whole life.

Jane Creswell, in *Coaching for Excellence*, describes the coachee's agenda as, "More than just his or her plan for a meeting. It conveys the fact that everything associated with coaching—the topic, the pace, the action, the evaluation—is centered around the PBC."[4]

There are many different ways to express what coaching looks like. Each one illustrates coaching in a way that I hope brings clarity and simplicity to the reader.

I have illustrated the coaching model using three funnels. There are seven stages to the model. My goal is to give you a physical picture that will give you a general track to follow as you coach.

---

[3] Adapted from: Laura Whitworth, Co-active Coaching (Mountain View, CA: Davies-Black, 2007), 3

[4] Creswell, Jane. The Complete Idiot's Guide to Coaching for Excellence. New York: Alpha Books, 2008. 11.

THE COACHING MODEL

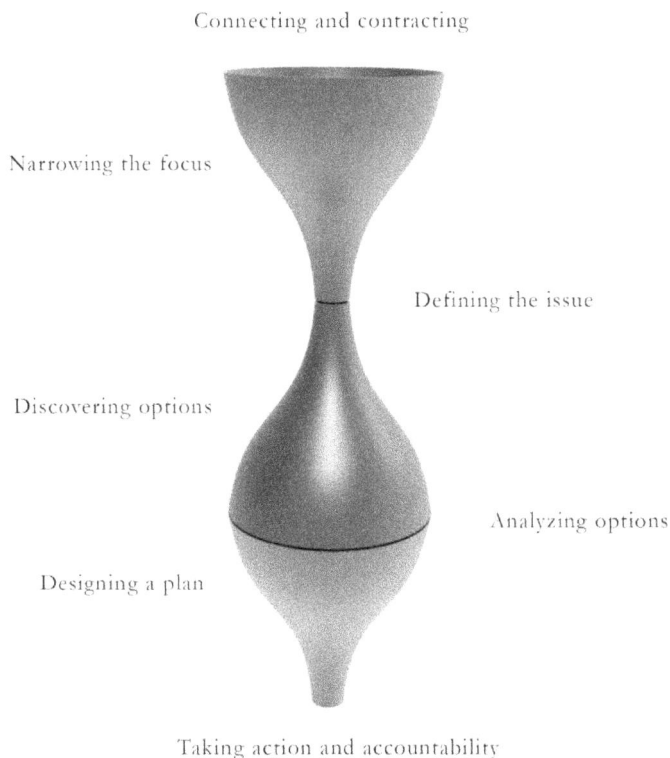

Connecting and contracting

Narrowing the focus

Defining the issue

Discovering options

Analyzing options

Designing a plan

Taking action and accountability

CONNECTING AND CONTRACTING

The first part of the coaching conversation begins with connecting. As a coach you need to reconnect, or connect for the first time, with the coachee. Simple questions like, "How are you doing?" or "What have you been encouraged by?" work well in this connecting process.

The second part of the coaching conversations is contracting. This is where we start to set the agenda with the coachee. Coaching is always looking forward with intentionality. Simple questions will help the coachee focus the conversation's results on moving forward while being intentional and strategic. Contracting questions might include the following:

- How can this conversation help move you forward?
- What would make today's conversation a success?
- When we are done, what do you need to take away?
- What do you want to address?

While working with beginning coaches, I notice this contracting step is rushed over and not clearly defined. This causes the coaching session to wander and often produces little progress.

NARROWING THE FOCUS

Once we know what the coachee wants to accomplish, it is time to explore the issue and helping the coachee discover all the dynamics surrounding it. Generally, a coaching topic is like a diamond, it has many facets. Each side is important and, if not explored fully, the coachee can miss important insights. Narrowing questions might include the following:

- What makes this topic important to you?
- What part of the situation have you not yet explored?
- If you could wave a magic wand, what would the end result look like?

- How does this relate to your values (life purpose)?

DEFINING THE ISSUE

It is in defining the issue we bring clarity to the real matter or situation the coachee wants to address. After spending time exploring all aspects, the coachee may see new parts of the issue he or she did not see earlier.

Sometimes the entire direction of the conversation can change at this point. What was important is now surpassed by new awareness and new desired outcomes. When we go slow discovering this direction, the rest of the coaching conversation seems to go much quicker.

- Which part of this issue do you want to address?
- Which part is still not clear?
- What are your personal values saying to you?
- How do you want to be seen by others?

DISCOVERING OPTIONS

Now is the time to help the coachee become creative and look at all available resources. Brainstorming, creating lists, checking with others, exploring past experiences and challenging assumptions are all powerful ways of helping the coachee discover new options.

The more options that are on the table, the better opportunity the coachee has of finding one that works and he or she is willing to commit to. When I ask for a list of options, I always ask for a minimum of five. The first one or two will be easy but not the best. With number three, the coachees will begin to think outside their box and create new solutions.

- What has worked for others?
- What are possible ways to get there?
- What options can you create?
- What else?

ANALYZING OPTIONS

Helping the coachee weigh each option will help bring clarity. The temptation is to interject judgments or personal opinions. This work of analyzing belongs to the coachee and only to the coachee.

While analyzing options, the role of the coach is to be sure the options align with the coachee's values and goals. Simple questions will help keep clarity in this area. Along with values, which option is doable and will it move the coachee forward?

- If you had your choice, what would you do?
- Where will this option lead you?
- What will you get?
- How does this line up with your personal values?

DESIGNING A PLAN

Once all options have been analyzed, the coachee is ready and equipped to design a plan of action. The most important ingredient of a plan is whether or not it is specific. Often plans are created with too large of steps and discourage the coachee from taking action.

When forming a plan, help the coachee answer the who, what, where, when and how questions. What action steps need to be taken? Who will take them? When will they be completed? How will they be accomplished?

- What will you do?
- When can you do it by?
- What steps will take you to your goal?
- What do you need to accomplish this?

TAKING ACTION AND ACCOUNTABILITY

Having an action plan does not guarantee success. There are often saboteurs lurking around the corner waiting to trip up the coachee: fear, lack of commitment, timing issues, personality quirks in the coachee or others, and a whole host of possibilities. It is important to address these up front.

I love the comics. Peanuts had a strip that spoke to the matter of knowing when you are successful. Charlie Brown was practicing archery in his back yard. Lucy stops by and wants Charlie Brown to demonstrate his skills. To her surprise, Charlie took the arrow, placed it on his bow and fired it into the fence. He then proceeded to draw a target around the arrow. Lucy could not help but question, "Charlie Brown, what are you doing?" Without any embarrassment he answered, "I'm making sure I never miss." Let's draw the target before we shoot the arrow.

- What might stop you?
- When will you start?
- How will you measure your progress?
- How will you know you have succeeded?

HOW DO YOU LEARN TO COACH?

The comment I hear over and over from students new to coaching is how hard it is to learn. Some classes I teach have students who are in the midst of counseling programs or have just graduated from one. The observation is always the same, "This is so different from counseling."

If it is so hard, what do I need to do to be a great coach? There are five ways to become a great coach. It is a combination of all five that will produce the necessary skills and mindset for exceptional coaching.

STUDY

Read five to ten books on coaching. Take courses offered locally or on the internet. When looking for good books or courses, it is wise to be cautious. Coaching is not regulated by any organizational or governmental body, this gives room for less-than-reputable people and schools to offer training that is not up to the quality you need to become an excellent coach.

I personally have interacted with coaches who were certified by some of these organizations and found their coaching skills lacking in every way.

OBSERVE

Find a setting where you can observe qualified coaches. There are some great coaches who are not certified with any group. However, again, be careful; bad habits are hard to unlearn. You can find qualified coaches at meetings of coaching associations. Look for International Coach Federation (ICF) certification.

BE COACHED

Get a coach if you want to be a coach. I have been involved with coaching since 2007, and have had a number of coaches. When I wrote my first book, I joined a writer's coaching group. Then I hired a book coach to help me finish strong. Today, I still have a business coach who is ICF certified.

COACH

Find friends or groups that will let you coach them. Just remember to do no harm. Experience is so important when it comes to coaching; exchange coaching with another person who is learning the art of being a coach. Peer coaching is a great way to practice and get coaching.

PRACTICE, PRACTICE AND PRACTICE

Like any new skill, it takes practice to develop it. I have practiced my coaching skills for years, with intentionality. I keep learning in every class I take, every class I teach, and every coaching session I am in. There is no perfect coaching conversation. You can always improve your skill set; this comes with practice.

In the next chapter we will explore the skills to gather information while coaching.

I have included additional resources to help you understand and excel at coaching. To download these resources go to billgraybill.com/IntroCoachingResources

Dr. Bill Graybill

5

START WITH GATHERING
INFORMATION

I was just beginning my coaching career, while loving the experience I was struggling with the process. I knew coaches asked questions, but creating a good question was difficult. I wanted someone to hand me a list of great questions and I could just pick the ones I wanted to use.

As I struggled to form questions, I realized I did not have a good grasp on the situation. I was so busy thinking about the next question I wasn't listening to the coachee. My inexperience highlights the importance of starting off with good input so that your output can be strong.

LISTENING

It all begins with good listening skills. And yes, most of us are poor listeners. Have you found yourself just waiting for the other person to use a period instead of a comma so you can tell them what you are thinking? We all have been guilty. We listen to respond, when we need to listen to understand.

There are three levels of listening, and the coach needs to operate in level two and three.

Level I listening is centered on, "What does this mean to me?" Listening at this level means the listener is paying more attention to his or her own judgments, opinions and feelings while driving his or her own agenda. Level I listening is acceptable for the coachee whose task is to look at themselves and their lives. They need to process, think about, feel and understand what is taking place inside.

Level II listening is focusing your awareness totally on the coachee and what they are saying. You're listening to their words, tone of voice and body language and are not distracted by your own thoughts and feelings. By listening at level II you can get a real understanding of where the coachee is "coming from," they feel understood, and the coach's own thoughts will not influence the coaching session.

Level III listening is often called "global listening." Here it is all about everything. When coaching at this level, you will be listening to everything available using intuition, emotional awareness, and sensing signals from your coachee's body language. You can gauge the energy of your coachee and their emotions as well as sensing what they are not saying. You will understand what they are thinking and feeling.

Tips for good listening:

- Stop talking
- Focus on the speaker

- Communicate your willingness to listen
- Remove distractions
- Lean into the speaker's point of view
- Be patient
- Be impartial and non-judgmental
- Listen for ideas, not just words
- Observe the non-verbal communication

OBSERVING

Careful observation is an essential coaching skill. It is vital to suspend judgment at this stage and not contaminate the observation process with your own prejudices and assumptions.

There are a number of things you can observe:

- Words that are often repeated
- Words that are missing or not said
- Facial expressions
- Change of energy
- Body language
- Reactions to questions or statements
- Presence

When you observe something, don't give it meaning, but hand it back to the coachee and ask for him or her to assign meaning. This keeps you out of the game and allows the coachee to fill in gaps or gain new awareness. This concept is illustrated on the next page with "The Ladder of Inference" diagram.

LADDER OF INFERENCE

Take Action

Adopt Beliefs

Draw Conclusions

Make Assumptions

Add Meanings

Select Data

Observe & Experience

Gap analysis is where you gain insight into the gap between what is desired and what is reality. This gap is discovered by exploring the two ends of the spectrum. You begin with the desired goal and then move to what is reality at the moment. This is used in managing employees and their performance.

It is also a good tool to have ready when the coachee lacks awareness of the difference between their goal and the present situation. As a coach, you may see the gap before the coachee. With this observation, you will be able to form questions to help the coachee discover the gap. Once this is accomplished, the coachee will be able to see clearly his target and can begin to work on the steps necessary to close the gap.

MEASURING PROGRESS

Another input you will need is the ability to measure progress and keep the coachee aware of the progress being made. If it is positive progress, it gives opportunity for the coach to give enthusiastic encouragement (output). A good coach will help the coachee celebrate the victories. Celebration is often overlooked by the coachee because they are focused on the target or end goal. It will help the coachee stay motivated when there are celebrations along the way.

What if the progress is not positive? Good question. This leads to several options. It is time to explore if the target is the right target for the coachee. Some targets are chosen because the coachee feels obligated or pressured to pick that particular target. Another option to explore is why the progress is not happening. Life situations, medical issues, conflict, and a million other things might be in the way, or the steps were too big and overwhelming. Having observed this lack of progress, it is the coach who must ask the coachee how he wants to deal with it.

CURIOSITY

To get good input you must stay curious. Curiosity is the coach's best friend. There is a big difference between conventional questions that elicit information and curious questions that evoke personal exploration. The following examples illustrate the differences between the two types of questions:[5]

Information Gathering	Curious
What topics will you include in the report?	What will finishing the report give you?
How much exercise do you need each week?	What would "being fit" look like for you?
What training options are available?	What do you want to know that you don't know today?

One of the ways I stay curious is that I begin with a statement, "I'm curious, tell me about…" If I know the answer, then I know I am not being curious but leading the coachee to a place that fits my agenda, not theirs.

INPUT FROM THE HOLY SPIRIT

As Christians, we can be intentional about tapping into the Holy Spirit. God is still active in the world, and especially in the lives of believers. While I believe He is active in all lives, believers have given Him a special invitation, and keep their ears open to Him.

---

[5] Laura Whitworth, Co-Active Coaching (Mountain View, CA.: Davies-Black, 2007), 70

Here are some tips for hearing the Holy Spirit during a coaching conversation, or at any time:

- Expect Him to be present and active
- Create an environment where He can be heard
- Discern how to handle what you hear
- Be ready to respond to His promptings

Let me just give this warning: this is not a license to tell the person what God is saying or to tell them what to do. In my experience, it is simply a question that I would never have thought of but it just pops into my mind. I usually explain that my question may seem strange but I sense I need to ask it.

The diagram on the next page illustrates this concept of including and being attentive to the Holy Spirit in a coaching conversation.

THE TWO-WAY CONVERSATION

The Coach   The Coachee

THE THREE-WAY CONVERSATION

The Holy Spirit

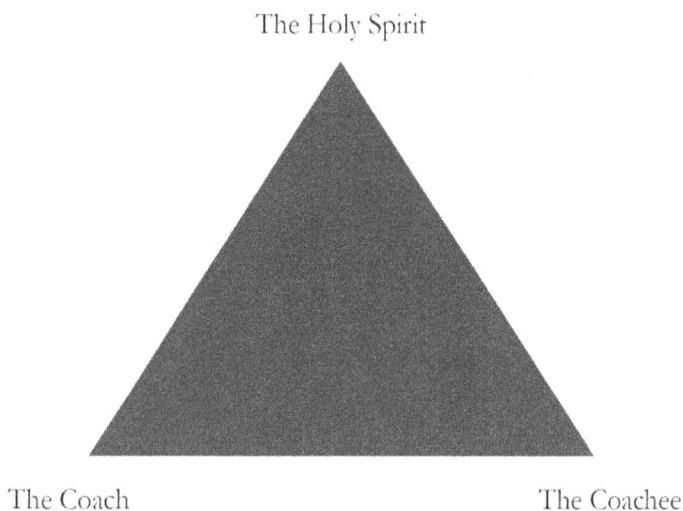

The Coach   The Coachee

Remember, before good questions can be created, it is necessary to become curious and help the coachee become curious. With good input you will be able to form the questions which spark new insights and awareness.

In the chapter we will move to asking powerful questions and other output skills

6

POWERFUL QUESTIONS

AND MORE

I sat in front of the Coaching 101 class and watched as the student sitting in front of me began to have tears trickle down her cheek. The last few questions were powerful and causing her to go deeper than she intended to go. I felt a little sorry for her but knew the class would go with her into areas fresh with new insights.

Good questions at the right time can evoke powerful emotions. I have a high batting average for touching sensitive areas when doing coaching demonstrations with female students. I know it is not me but rather the power of a good question at the right time.

POWERFUL QUESTIONS

The purpose of the question is not to gain information but to help the coachee capture new insights and perspectives. The coach is listening to the answers in order to know what question the coachee needs next. If you are asking questions to satisfy your own curiosity, you will miss the next good question.

There are two types of questions: open questions and closed questions. A closed question is answered by a simple "Yes," a "No," or a brief answer. Open questions are questions encouraging a dialogue or in-depth answer. With an open question, the coachee is free to explore outside the box and gain new ideas.

The strength of powerful questions is measured by the impact it has on the coachee. Asking the right questions can cause someone to think imaginatively about what could be possible. Making a statement causes people to judge (agree or disagree with your statement) and can bring up resistance. When you ask the right question, you help people tap into the part of the brain that is creative.

A powerful question can:

- Gain information
- Promote discovery
- Bring clarification
- Probe
- Generate options
- Uncover obstacles
- Determine next steps

Powerful questions are concise, clear and relevant, needing no explanation or elaboration. It is best to keep the number of questions limited during a coaching conversation. A good coach will only talk about 20 percent of the time and give the other 80 percent to the coachee.

Here are four rules for asking powerful questions:

- As simple as possible
- Don't give advice
- Don't tell people something they can discover on their own
- Don't fix the problem for them.

AVERAGE VS. POWERFUL QUESTIONS[6]

Average	Powerful
What does your to-do list look like today? (no new info for the coachee)	What are the three to-do's on your list with the greatest impact?
Can you do that? (closed question)	What will it take to do that?
Why did you do that? (creates defensiveness)	What were your underlying assumptions? Which of those assumptions need challenging?
Have you tried this idea? (coach's idea)	What can you try next?
How might changing your mind help you move forward? (leading question, maybe their mind doesn't need to change)	How do you need to think about this to move forward?

---

[6] Adapted from Jane Creswell, Coaching for Excellence (New York, NY.: Alpha, 2008), 49

A couple of years ago I wanted to gather a list of powerful questions. As a member of LinkedIn, I went to a coaching group and requested coaches to add their best questions to the list. Here is a sample of "Best Powerful Questions."

- What would you do if you were 10 times bolder? (Used to help clients see around the obstacles)
- What does success look like?
- What is most important to you?
- If nothing changes, what will that cost you?
- What else?
- What assumptions are you making?

Notice how short, simple, and direct they are. They are created, and asked, to help the coachee gain new awareness.

MAKING STATEMENTS

There is a time in coaching to make statements and give input to the coachee. When the need arises to make a statement, it needs to be clear and concise with the goal of helping the coachee move forward.

The first type of statement is "reframing." When a coachee is stuck in how they are seeing a situation or experience, the coach can help move them forward by reframing. This provides a fresh perspective and a sense of renewed possibility.

Reframing is looking on the bright side of things. It takes real pieces of the coachee's situation and shifts the perspective to show an opportunity that is being missed.

Reframing changes the theme from "my calendar is running my life" to "I am running my life."

"Summarizing" is another statement available to coaches. This is simply taking what the coachee has said and repackaging it to be a brief overview. A couple things can happen when summarizing is used. The coachee might agree with the summarization and realize he or she did not mean what they said. The repackaging and handing it back to the coachee can be a powerful way of helping the coachee see beyond the details where they are stuck.

Summarizing may comprise:

- the last few sentences the coachee has spoken
- an earlier part of a conversation
- a review of the whole current coaching conversation
- a reminder of how far the client has come during the whole coaching conversation

Here are some simple rules for summarizing:

- Summarize the main ideas
- Look for what the person is trying to communicate
- Make the summary shorter than the original statement
- Make notes if you need to do so

"Mirroring" is a valuable statement tool. Mirroring is repeating the coachee's exact words back to them. This strengthens the relationship and reassures the coachee that you are listening and what they have said is worthwhile.

When a coachee hears their own words coming back from the coach, they feel validated and encouraged to move forward. To be effective, the coach needs to feed the words back in the same way they were spoken.

Another statement is "paraphrasing." This is when you repeat back to the coachee what they said, using your own words. This is effective in helping the coachee find the words which enables them to express themselves accurately.

Here are some simple rules when paraphrasing:

- Put the focus on what the other person implied, not what you wanted him or her to imply.
- Make the paraphrase a question, "Are you saying…?"
- Make the paraphrase shorter than the original statement.
- Paraphrase without judgment.

ENCOURAGEMENT

Aidan O'Flynn, a Rugby coach, shared this insight that also applies to this style of coaching. "In my work with young pros as Personal Development Academy Coach, the issues that often arise are: fear of failure, negative or unsupportive self-talk, poor ability to recover after setbacks and mistakes, lack of intrinsic motivation, and fragile confidence."[7]

---

[7] http://www.independent.ie/sport/rugby/why-coaching-should-be-about-encouragement-30651824.html

Encouragement can help the coachee overcome several different obstacles. As Aidan O'Flynn pointed out, people struggle with overcoming their self-image; they need something to help them take the first step. As a coach, your confidence in them and your encouragement may be the key to their commitment to take action.

If they are facing a particularly difficult decision or action, your encouragement may be the ticket. Everyone needs encouragement, and is looking for it. Have you ever heard someone say they have had too much encouragement or affirmation? Nor have I.

SILENCE

Silence is a gift you can give to your coachee. It gives them space and permission to go deeper in their thought process. If you are asking powerful questions, then they are encountering new information, thoughts and options. They need time to process this without feeling the pressure to keep the conversation going.

There is a 14-second rule when it comes to silence. People can't stand silence for more that 14 seconds...someone will speak, out of their discomfort. When you learn to live in the moment and let silence be a part of that moment, you are giving a very valuable and rare gift.

In the next chapter we will look at how to move to action and create an Action Plan.

7

TIME FOR ACTION

I had been working hard with Bonnie, helping her discover what she wanted her life to look like in three years. Having just come through a divorce and losing the security her marriage afforded her, Bonnie's future was uncertain and she was lost in her circumstances. Not knowing what to do next, she reached out for help and found a coach to help her define her "new normal."

Now that we knew what Bonnie wanted her new normal to be, it was time to create a roadmap. How would she make the changes and decisions necessary to arrive at her three-year destination? What choices were before her? How would she make these choices? What might derail her plans? What kind of a person would she need to be to make this journey? Who would hold her accountable to carry out her decisions? This next stage would be just as hard as the first.

DISCOVER OPTIONS

The purpose of discovering options is to create a list of as many alternative courses of action as possible. It is not about finding the "right action," but looking for every possible alternative. The quantity of options is more important than the quality and feasibility, at this point. The very act of creating a slew of options will stimulate the creative side of the brain, and new possibilities will be uncovered.

There are several enemies of discovering the available options. These will keep a coachee stuck and unable to see beyond the present circumstances. Here are three big ones:

- Assumptions—coming to conclusions without the necessary information to make an informed decision. Accepting something as true without proof.
- In the box thinking—thinking that is limited by preconceived ideas or false belief. Unable to see past the way things are done or have been done.
- Negative mindset—Believing something will not work before giving it a chance. Always looking for the reason why you might fail, or what you try will fail.

A coach's job is to question and help the coachee test these obstacles to see if they are really true. One of the reasons I enjoy coaching is watching a person discover that the limiting factor in their life is a deception. Now they are free to make new choices, no longer limited by fictional obstacles.

The challenge for the coach is to allow the coachee to find or create the options. There is something in every one of us that wants to solve the problem for the other person. The coachee knows much more than you do, so your job is to help them uncover what they already know. Create an environment where the coachee feels safe to explore ideas, even when they seem unusual or odd.

You help the coachee by asking probing questions, allowing them to discover new information or possible actions. A good question will be one where you and the coachee do not know the answer. Generally speaking, it will be a short and concise question. In this activity, I like to have the coachees create lists. I require the list to include five things. If they come up with five quickly, I will add another three or four. The best ideas are usually not the first ones on the list.

Here is a list of questions that can be used in helping the coachee uncover new options:

- If you could do anything you wanted, what would you do?
- What options can you create?
- What options have you not yet explored?
- What else?
- What is just one more possibility?
- What do you know that has worked for others?

FORM A PLAN

There are people who resist making a plan because they feel it will limit them and stifle their creativity. Nonsense. Planning and having a plan provides and promotes freedom. It frees you to move forward without reservation or fear. Forming a plan is essential for finding success.

If the goal or task is big, and might seem overwhelming, break the goal into small increments and create a plan for each step. A good action plan needs to be realistic and functional.

Don't forget to take into account current life circumstances. Be sure it is specific and concrete.

When considering which options to include in the plan, consider the following:

- Adaptability
- Affordability
- Time constraints
- Value alignment
- Availability of resources

Here are some possible questions to use when helping a coachee create an action plan:

- What is your game plan?
- Now what?
- How do you suppose you could improve the situation?
- What resources do you need?
- Who else needs to be involved?

Gary Collins, in his book, *Christian Coaching*, gives this seven-step process for creating a plan:[8]

Step 1—Agree on the end result (the desired outcome).

Step 2—Put this on paper. You can revise it later.

Step 3—Start with the desired outcomes. Then, working backward, mutually brainstorm about some possible interim goals.

---

[8] Gary R. Collins, Christian Coaching (Colorado Springs, CO: NavPress, 2001), 154

Step 4—Agree about which of these alternative, interim goals you will pursue.

Step 5—Arrange the goals in order from the first and most realistic to the end result.

Step 6—Put this list on paper.

Step 7—Try to answer some tough questions, especially as you consider the first one or two goals:

- Is the goal so specific that you know exactly what needs to be done?
- What's the first step? (Start with the first goal.)
- When you reach the goal, how will you know you're there?
- What will be the specific evidence that you've succeeded?

REMOVE OBSTACLES

Now is the time to address obstacles and create ways to overcome them. Your job as a coach will be to help the coachee isolate obstacles and be proactive. Surprises will always pop up; it is best to anticipate and plan for them.

Tips for managing unforeseen obstacles:

- Step back emotionally
- Breathe
- Don't panic
- Coach through the obstacle
- Adjust action as necessary
- Keep focus on overall goal

Here are a few questions to get you started with addressing obstacles:

- What might stop you from completing your plan?
- Where do you feel internal resistance?
- Where might external resistance come from?
- How will you know you are not making progress?
- How will you handle unexpected obstacles?

ACCOUNTABILITY

People do what is inspected, not expected. That is the principal reason we have accountability. There is a second reason, measuring progress. What was accomplished? What is the next step? Where are we in the process?

Being accountable is part of the coaching process and, like all the other stages, this stage is in the hands of the coachee. They know what motivates them to action. When "they" form the accountability structure, they will embrace it willingly.

Good accountability structure energizes and motivates, instead of creating the feeling of being "watched over" or controlled. The purpose of accountability is to supply energy for change. I often have the coachee design their own homework and accountability structure. I shy away from being the accountability partner and have them find someone else who will hold them accountable. This reduces the guilt factor in our relationship.

Here are some accountability questions to spark your imagination:

- How would you like to be held accountable?
- What are you going to accomplish?
- When will you complete this?

- What actions will you take to complete this?
- Who can you ask to hold you accountable?

In the next chapter we will explore what a Life Coach does.

I have included additional resources to help you understand and excel at coaching. To download these resources go to billgraybill.com/IntroCoachingResources

8

THE CRAFT OF

LIFE COACHING

Life coaching. Buzz word or valid career? Great question! Let's look at what a life coach accomplishes, then you decide if it is a valid line of work.

THE VALUE OF LIFE COACHING

In a blog post on Life Coach Spotter[9] we learn that a life coach helps you:

- Get crystal clear on what you really want in your life
- Uncover what's holding you back from achieving your vision for yourself
- Take action steps to achieve your vision by supporting you and keeping you accountable

---

[9] http://www.lifecoachspotter.com/what-does-life-coach-do/

Three steps that take a person from a present reality to a desired future reality. This is a simple, clear and concise picture of what life coaching is. There are a lot more aspects to it but, in a nutshell, this gives us a picture to answer the question: buzz word or valid career? Is helping someone move forward and obtain their desired goals worth monetary reward? I think it is.

In reality, all coaching is life coaching. I have a business coach named Tim. When we work together, he is centering in on how I live my life as a coach who is building a business. Sometimes we talk about relationships in the business. Other times we talk about how I am going to achieve a specific business goal. Then there are the coaching sessions around what goals do I have for the next six months. This is how life and coaching intersect. No matter the niche name we put on it, it is really coaching about how we are going to live life.

WHO IS COACHABLE

Jane Creswell, MCC, in her book, *The Complete Idiot's Guide to Coaching for Excellence*, deals with the key issue of coachability. Is everyone coachable? Does everyone want to be coached? Will they make a good coachee or client? These are important questions needing an answer, before you start attempting to coach someone.

Jane gives this definition, "Coachability is a combination of willingness, readiness, and respect for the coaching process. People go in and out of coachability based on their personality and circumstances."[10]

---

[10] Creswell, Jane. The Complete Idiot's Guide to Coaching for Excellence. New York: Alpha Books, 2008. 64.

She goes on to list the following 10 characteristics, indicating that if someone has at least three of these, coaching will be able to help them:

- The person has potential but has maxed out on current resources.
- The person demonstrates a desire to continue growing in his or her current job and beyond.
- The person has goals and is willing to make life changes to meet those goals.
- The person is action-oriented and continues to make forward progress.
- The person implements change well, and is often the first to attempt new processes and learn new skills.
- The person learns from others and uses new information to continue to grow.
- The person thrives when given new, challenging assignments.
- The person has difficulty balancing work and personal/family time.
- The person has been doing the same thing the same way for too long and definitely needs a boost to move out of stagnation.
- The person has good ideas but has difficulty moving from idea to implementation.

HELPING SOMEONE BE COACHABLE
I want to give you the top four actions I have found to help people be good clients.

Pick the Right Client
The first action is to pick the right client. Not everyone wants to be coached for various reasons. A spouse may not want to be coached by their marriage partner. In business, supervisors may resist coaching from a lower-ranked employee. Sometimes employees will refuse to give it their all because it has been mandated by their employer.

When picking a client, I want to get to know them well enough to ask questions based on the ten characteristics in the last section. I look for what is motivating them. Are they choosing coaching or is it being forced on them? I do not coach everyone who expresses interest in being coached. Some people, while being interested, are not motivated to the degree necessary to do the work of growing and changing.

Personal Cost and Commitment
Once I have determined that someone has potential as a coachee, I require some sort of personal cost and commitment. This is usually in the form of monetary investment. In other words, I make them pay for coaching. When I began coaching I would coach for free, thinking everyone wanted this magic I had discovered. I soon learned that unless they have "skin in the game," they will not give the needed effort and commitment.

Prep Forms
My third action is to use coaching prep forms. I have a long one I use at the very beginning of the coaching relationship and a five question prep form that is filled out before each session. This helps the coachee come to the session ready to work and move forward. Without results, people lose interest and do not find adequate return on their investment of time and resources.

In this same context, I also use a form that helps them internalize what they learned and committed to during our time together. I ask them to take 15-minutes after each session to consider what happened and to deepen the learning. Without this time, clients would rush back into the business of the day and lose much of what they accomplished. I get lots of positive feedback concerning this practice.

Professional Presentation of Coaching
The fourth action I take is to maintain a professional presentation of coaching. I accomplish this by four commitments:

- I am clear about which hat I am wearing when I interact with people. If I am in a casual setting and it seems coaching might be helpful, I ask permission to put on my coach hat.
- During a coaching session I might find a time when my pastoral or consultant hat is a better choice. I ask permission to change hats.
- I protect confidentiality. People want to know their story is safe with the coach. I have clients who want me to use their story to help others. Even with permission, I change names and situations to give them a sense of safety.
- I treat each person and what they share with deep respect. They are not objects or simply vehicles to get a paycheck. They are real people with hurts, dreams, needs and desires.

KNOWING THE BIG PICTURE
Every successful road trip starts with picking a destination. Every successful coaching journey must include identifying a target or desired future. When someone invests time, energy and money, they want tangible long-term results.

You will not necessarily identify the goal during your first appointment, but within a few sessions you and the client should understand the long-term target. I find the way to the goal is seldom straight, but has many side trips to remove roadblocks caused by crises along the way.

Because the trip is not straight and quick, the client will lose focus and hope unless there is a clear target. Since the road twists and turns, expect the journey to take longer than first anticipated. I warn the client about this reality before we begin.

Just this morning I got an email from a client referencing our call later this week. He indicated that he was not sure what to bring to the conversation. I simply referred him back to working on the big picture. Why this confusion? We had spent several sessions working on a crisis and he lost sight of the big picture.

WHEN IS LIFE COACHING NOT COACHING

There are many actions that can undermine and damage a coaching relationship. I want to explore four of them here.

- You have quit coaching when you impose the agenda. When I work with a client, I often review what we have worked on by referring to the coaching prep form they filled out and sent to me. I then move to handing the session to them with a question, asking them what would be helpful for them to accomplish during our time together.

- You have quit coaching when you know the answer you want the client to know. We live in a "fix it" world, where fixing each other is an automatic response. I examine my questions carefully and, if I already know the answer, I reject the question. My goal is to remain curious and help the client maintain a sense of curiosity, which will lead them to new awareness and better understanding, and ultimately a better solution.

- You have quit coaching when you make judgments about what the client brings to the session. Every coach is tempted to make judgment calls. We all have our own values and filters we use to see the world around us. Coaching requires the coach to lay down those judgments and allow the client to freely explore their situations, knowing they will not be judged. This may require careful selection of clients if your sensitivities are easily offended.

- You have quit coaching when you lead the client to the conclusion you feel is best for them. Another aspect of the "fix it" world we live in is the desire to lead the client to the "right decision or action." This is especially true if you have a caring and concerned heart. Coaching is not for the weak-hearted. A coach is not called to do the fixing, but to help the client discover their own answers. At the very center of coaching is the belief that the client has the best answers to their situation. It is important that the coach believes in the abilities of the client to be creative and find their own best way to the target. The coach's job is to help the client unleash their creativity.

THE WHEEL OF LIFE

To help clients better determine their journey, I use the Wheel of Life exercise. This is a common instrument and has many variations. I personally use four different wheels depending on the setting and needs of my client. I have provided this sample from my own library. See the Appendix A for a complete Wheel of Life exercise.

WHEEL OF LIFE

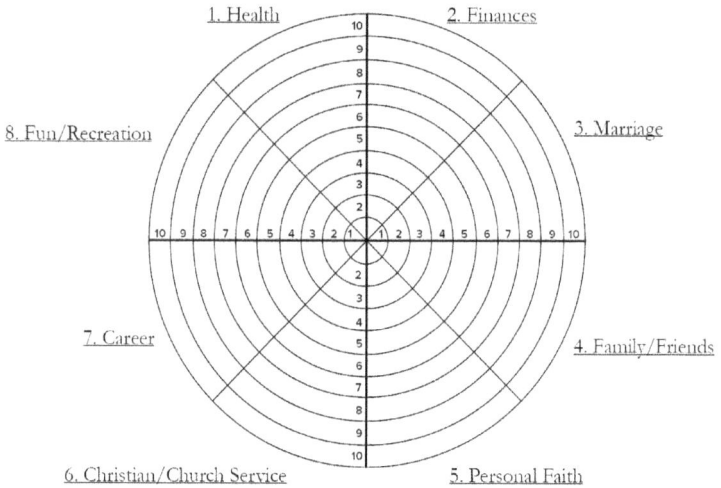

In the next chapter, we will explore coaching around faith and discipleship.

9

FAITH AND DISCIPLESHIP

COACHING

Tom sat across the desk from me and explained how he was not growing spiritually. It was not a new story but one that always makes me disappointed and sad. Tom was a product of our cookie-cutter-discipleship program. You may know the one I am talking about; take a book, answer the questions by looking up scripture, and learn some new information.

I looked at Tom and asked a simple question, "If you could take a huge step forward in spiritual growth, what would be different?" He pondered the question for almost a full minute and then began to paint of picture of what he wanted his spiritual life to look like. Answering a simple question, and working toward that answer through coaching, Tom began an exciting new faith adventure, which continues today.

WHAT MAKES FAITH COACHING DIFFERENT

The authors of *Faith Coaching; A Conversational Approach to Helping Others Move Forward in Faith,* share a crucial insight concerning the nature of faith coaching.[11] They write that faith coaching "is really about participating in the work of the Spirit by being a paraclete for people who want to bear more fully the image of God."

The first contrast is who gets to set the agenda. Is it going to be the coachee's agenda or God's agenda? Faith coaching gives deference to what the coachee senses God is wanting. While this may seem obvious and simple, I find that surrendering a personal agenda is often difficult, and requires intense spiritual work.

Part of the faith coaching process may include discerning what God's agenda is. While we know what His written word says to us, it is recognizing how the word needs to be applied that proves elusive and difficult to know. Faith coaching gives credence to this dilemma and addresses it head on.

The second distinction can center on the big picture of destiny. As Christians, we believe people have a destiny and purpose in the plan of God. It is this belief that helps drive faith coaching to see a bigger picture than just a measure of success or happiness.

Faith coaching helps the coachee be aware of how his decisions, plans and paths relate to this perceived destiny or over-arching purpose. A simple question, such as, "Where is God in that?" can help the coachee keep his eyes on the big picture.

---

[11] Hall, Chad W., and Bill Copper. Faith Coaching: A Conversational Approach to Helping Others Move Forward in Faith. Hickory, N.C.: Coach Approach Ministries, 2009. 8.

The third unique area is the focus on spiritual transformation.[12] Anything less that an authentic and deep reshaping of the inner person is short-changing the faith coaching ideal.

There is something in us that wants our actions to change, while resisting the change inside. I think this might come from the fact that in changing we are leaving behind a comfortable way of living. One that we have become used to and see it as who we are. Change requires we admit our core being is defective and needs renewing. Intellectually it is an easy confession, but it causes internal protest.

FAITH COACHING IS DYNAMIC

By dynamic I mean full of life, change and growth. It is filled with new discoveries of spiritual truth, application of that truth and life-changing encounters with a living God. There is excitement, amusement and delight in the journey.

Religious leaders often hold agendas for those they lead. Faith coaching looks beyond the established path to the deep path within. When you see my actions, you can conclude you know what I need to change. When I know my motivations, I often come to a different conclusion of what is needed.

I love information. I own a library of over 4,000 books and have made each one my friend. But information is not enough. Faith coaching is not about information, but transformation. It is in this transformational changing that a new person is found within.

---

[12] Romans 8:29

Faith coaching is the intentional inclusion of the Holy Spirit in the coaching process. Rather than looking only to a set of questions and a coaching model, the guidance of the Spirit is sought and embraced. The life of the Spirit is found at the center of the coaching.

THE THREE-WAY CONVERSATION

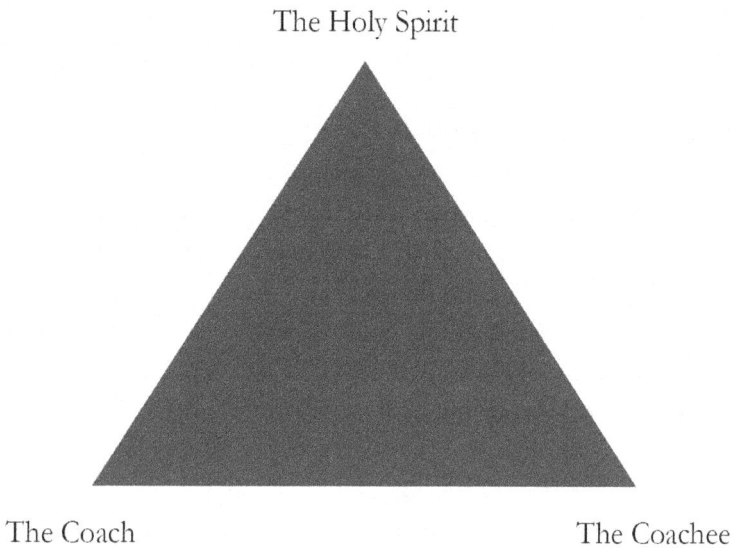

The Holy Spirit

The Coach   The Coachee

THE PARABLE OF THE SOILS

The Bible gives us four types of people whom we may coach, or attempt to coach. Each one is at a different place in life and therefore needs to be coached with wisdom, insight, and dependence on the Holy Spirit.

Some see this box as explaining where people are, with the expectation they will stay in their box. Others see this as a pathway of spiritual growth. Everyone is in a box, on a journey toward box 4. As a coach, I want to see people on a journey of change, not stuck in their present situation forever.

Look over the diagram on the next page. It is based on all three accounts of the parable of the soils as told by Jesus in the Gospels of Matthew, Mark and Luke.

BOX 1   BOX 2

The Path	The Rocks
Hear	No Nutrients
No Penetration	No Roots
STOLEN	WITHERS WHEN TESTED
The Thorns	**The Good Soil**
Worries	Hears
Riches	Good Heart
Pleasures	Understands
CHOKED OUT	PRODUCTIVE

BOX 3   BOX 4

One way to use this diagram in coaching would be to share it with the coachee.

- Have them determine where they might be presently.
- Explore with them what each box might look like in their life.
- How do they feel about where they are?
- If they were to move toward box 4, how would that affect others in their life?
- Have them pretend they are in box 4. How does that feel? What is different?

Each box can be explored individually, depending on where the coachee sees themselves. Here are some possible questions for each box:

Box 1: The Path
- Draw a picture of what the path might look like in your life. Now explore as many aspects of the path that you can think of.
- What is hard?
- What is scary about being in box 1?
- What might keep you there?
- What feelings does the word 'stolen' bring up?
- Create your own questions to help the coachee find their way out of the box.

Box 2: The Rocks
- What nutrients might be missing?
- What might the rocks represent in your life?
- Picture yourself as the rocky soil. What do you see? Feel?

- How do others see you as the rocky soil?
- What tests might come your way?
- Create your own questions to help the coachee find their way out of the box.

Box 3: The Thorns
- What makes this box frightening to you? To others for you?
- What is attractive in this box?
- Of the three characteristics, how is the one with the greatest pull affecting you?
- How might others describe you in this box?
- What happens if you do nothing?
- Create your own questions to help the coachee find their way out of the box.

Box 4: The Good Soil
- What constitutes good soil?
- How do you see yourself relating to this box?
- What might degrade this soil in your life?
- What could be strengthened in your life concerning this box?
- How do you see yourself productive?
- Create your own questions to help the coachee find their way out of the box.

As you look over this list of questions, I trust you are not limited by them. My hope is that they will spark your creativity to come up with your own questions.

THE IMPORTANCE OF VALUES

Faith coaching gives great opportunities to explore values and priorities. I often explore this area at the beginning of the coaching relationship. Once the coachee's values have been established, it gives a foundation for future decisions.

Part of coaching is the skill of challenging the coachee during the decision-making process. I have watched coachees make a decision which violates their values. With this value foundation in place, I have opportunity to ask how that choice lines up with their values.

To establish a coachee's values I have developed my own value assessment. While this one has been crafted by myself, there are many variations available on the internet. I have included my version in Appendix B. Feel free to customize it to fit your needs.

POSSIBLE TOPICS FOR FAITH COACHING

I have created a short list of possible subjects to coach in this area. There is no limit to this list, but it will give you an idea of how varied it can be. Each one of these topics can be subdivided into many categories.

- Parenting
- Spiritual growth
- Church planting
- Working with volunteers
- Effective ministry
- Salvation
- Marriage
- Missions
- Spiritual dryness
- Discipleship

- End of life
- Capital fundraising
- Building program
- Staff development
- Conflict resolution
- Team building

The list is endless when you consider all the sub-categories. The need is great within the church for quality coaching. There is set before us an opportunity to make a difference in the culture of the church.

In the next chapter, we will look at the very difficult but exciting subject of coaching conflict.

I have included additional resources to help you understand and excel at coaching. To download these resources go to billgraybill.com/IntroCoachingResources

Dr. Bill Graybill

10

COACHING CONFLICT

Sarah's voice was shrill, revealing the stress she was feeling. As I worked to calm her down, I knew her work situation was tough and conflict common. After allowing Sarah to vent her emotions, we got down to business. It was time to help her discover her choices and actions that fueled the blowup.

As our phone session came to an end, Sarah was ready to own her actions and admit to herself that she was at the center of the conflict. She knew what was required to heal the hurts her words had inflicted. With courage and determination, Sarah hung up the phone and walked down the hall to apologize and ask for forgiveness. It had been a tense call but, with simple questions, Sarah was able to gain new awareness about her actions.

My coaching niche is conflict resolution and organizational health. With that in mind, I look forward to writing this chapter and sharing some of the insights I have gained over the last two decades I have been involved with the subject of conflict resolution.

WHY RELATIONSHIPS ARE IMPORTANT

Conflict is about people frustrating other people by their actions. It is that simple. The key to resolving conflict begins by helping people, who have broken relationships, heal hurts and restore the relationship.

Restore relationships and find better solutions.

Most people see conflict resolution as finding solutions. They start by looking at actions. What actions caused the conflict? What actions are needed to find a solution acceptable to all involved? Seldom does this work. While the immediate problem is solved, the broken relationship, and hurt feelings, will cause further trouble down the road.

Conflict coaching is content-rich coaching, which means there will be some information and teaching taking place during the coaching conversation. Most people don't have the skills to resolve conflict well. We help them with the skills and they determine how and when they will use those skills.

I always start by exploring the relational side of the equation. What's broken? Who's hurt? What does that feel like for the other person? What might they tell me?

SELF-AWARENESS

Self-awareness and gold have two characteristics in common: both are valuable, and everyone could use more.

Jesus addresses this lack when he says, "First take the plank out of your own eye, and then you will see clearly to remove the speck from your brother's eye."[13]

---

[13] Matthew 7:5

The dictionary's definition of self-awareness is the "conscious knowledge of one's own character, feelings, motives, and desires." When it comes to conflict, most people are totally lacking in self-awareness. They give mental assent to the fact of their own imperfections, but emotionally it is another story.

Some areas where self-awareness may be lacking are as follows:
- How they handle conflict
- What is their level of anger
- How important is the issue at hand
- What insights are found in scripture
- How their attitude affects the conflict
- What they bring to the conflict
- How the other person sees them and the issue at hand
- What kind of person do they need to be to resolve the conflict

The process of helping people gain a clear perspective on the circumstances while embroiled in conflict is vital to the healing of relationships and redemptive conflict resolution. The process I have proposed will address self-awareness in a straight forward manner and give good results.

The important point to make here is the key to resolving conflict always starts with "me." Until I accept that fact, successful resolution will be elusive. Resist the "me" factor and you will miss the path necessary to healing relationships and finding powerful solutions.

The 5-Step Model
Step 1: Prayer
While prayer seems to be obvious to Christians, it is generally reserved for crisis situations. How many times have you heard, "Well, I've tried everything else, I better pray."

Now I am not saying you will be overt in this matter of prayer, but be aware of how prayer is being embraced by the coachee.

There are many places in coaching conflict where it is easy and appropriate to bring in the subject of prayer.

Step 2: Overlook
Most people ignore conflict hoping it will go away. It never does. This is why we need to differentiate between "ignoring" and "overlooking."

To ignore: To refuse to pay attention to

To overlook: To rise above and look over

You practice "overlooking" by extending grace because God extends grace to you. When you choose to overlook, you then need to change your attitude. Saying, "everything is okay," and still having a poor attitude is not overlooking an offense.

If it is possible to overlook the offense and change one's attitude, then there is no need to go further; the conflict has been resolved. However, there are times you can't overlook the offense or actions. It is important to know when "overlooking" is appropriate or when it is necessary to go on to the next step. Here is a simple question to ask: "Will this cause me to feel differently about the other person for more than a short period of time?" If this question is answered in the affirmative, then it is time to move forward to steps 3 through 5.

Step 3: Self-examination
One of the hardest parts of redemptive conflict resolution is getting people to own their own stuff. The first reaction is to go and show the other person where they are wrong.

One of the most important steps is understanding how you contributed to the conflict and damaged relationships. This "self-inspection" is the first step when you want to go to the other person to address the conflict.

What do people bring to the conflict that they often fail to notice? Here is a partial list often overlooked:

- Uncontrolled tongue
- Unfulfilled responsibilities
- Culture clashes
- Mismanaged expectations
- Unmanaged anger

Until a person is willing to accept what they bring to the conflict, there is no possibility of redemptive resolution. You might find agreement on what actions need to be taken, but the healing of the relationship will be missing.

Step 4: Communicate to restore broken relationships
There are two key actions that need to take place when restoring broken relationships: confession and forgiveness. The first action is confession.

Here are six principles of a good confession:

- Accept responsibility.
- Don't blame-shift by using the words If, But or Maybe.
- Be quick to admit you are wrong with an apology.
  - A compelling apology will go a long ways in helping the other person re-engage in the resolution process. It will contain the following four components:
    - Be specific in how attitudes were wrong.
    - Be specific in how actions were wrong.
    - Be specific in how words were wrong.
    - Be specific in asking for forgiveness.

The purpose of confession is to convey to the other person a clear understanding that their feelings have been hurt, damage has been done, and your desire to heal the relationship. Some people expect to get an apology in return. A good confession expects nothing in return but wants to heal what has been broken.

The second action is forgiveness. Forgiveness can be extended anytime. The coachee does not need to even interact with the other person.

Here are five principles to help one step into forgiveness:

- Forgiveness is not about, or defined by, feelings, forgetting or excusing.
- Forgiveness is a decision. It is a decision to release the offender from your judgment and trusting God to do what is right and just. (See Matthew 6:14-15)
- You are to forgive just as Jesus forgave you. How did He forgive you?
  - Completely
  - Unconditionally
  - Eternally
- When you forgive or release someone, you are releasing them from your judgment and your punishment. You are entrusting them to God, their only true judge.
- After releasing someone who has hurt you deeply, you need to continually release them every time you think of the situation. The pain does not leave immediately, but will lessen if you are faithful to your commitment to release them and trust God.

Here is a sample prayer that may help the client put it all together: Dear God, because you have forgiven me, I now extend forgiveness to _____. I release _____ from my judgment and trust you to do what is right and just. I give up my right to seek revenge, believing that you are the Judge who judges all men with truth and justice.

Step 5: Identify and implement a strategy to address systemic problems

When it comes to helping a client chart a course of action, the options are unlimited. In redemptive conflict resolution, the emphasis is on rebuilding broken relationships before finding solutions.

The temptation is to move to finding solutions before attending to the relationship aspect of the conflict. The following are possible, and often necessary actions:

- Forgiveness
- Confrontation
- Attitude change
- Culture shift
- New systems
- See people, not problems
- Team understanding (assessments)
- Re-organization (Move or Remove)
- Clarity of Purpose, Vision and Strategy
- Outside help

Due to the limitations of this chapter the treatment of coaching conflict is brief. To find more information on this topic, check out the following resources:

- My book on this subject: Resolve Conflict God's Way; The Skills You Need to Make Peace
- My course on coaching conflict: CAM 530 at Coach Approach Ministries or contact me directly
- My website with additional resources: www.peacementors.com

In the next chapter we will explore the exciting world of group coaching.

Dr. Bill Graybill

11

COACHING IN A GROUP

The phone went silent. In a few moments I heard Cindy's voice expressing thanks to the other callers on the group coaching call. She choked up as words of appreciation began to flow. There were five of us on the call, four coachees and one coach, me. It was an intense call with Cindy expressing discouragement and wanting to quit her role in children's ministry. She was hopeless with no idea about how to make some necessary changes. Without the adjustments, she saw disaster around the corner for her and the entire children's ministry.

It was the magic of the group working together and helping each other that gave Cindy her moment of hope. As the group explored her struggles together, with compassion and empathy, Cindy saw where she could make decisions and open the doors needed for change. While I am a good coach, it was the group dynamic, working together, that Cindy needed to have her breakthrough.

WHAT IS GROUP COACHING

I was first exposed to group coaching when I took a class taught by Ginger Cockerham. It was nine months in length, meeting every week. She is one of the foremost experts and practitioners of group coaching. She coaches financial advisors and others in the financial service field.

Ginger gives the following definition for group coaching: it "is a facilitated group process led by a skilled professional coach and created with the intention of maximizing the combined energy, experience, and wisdom of the individuals who choose to join in order to achieve organizational objectives or individual goals."[14]

While this seems a bit formal, it makes very clear some key aspects of group coaching:

- Skilled leadership in the person of a trained coach
- Intentionally in the coaching process
- Draws the building blocks from the group
- Goals can be organizational or individual

Group coaching is on the rise with professional coaching, and with good reason. Let me share some of the benefits of coaching in a group:

- The synergy of a group is greater than one-on-one coaching.
- You can accomplish more in less time within an organization.
- You are more effective with your time and have a wider range of influence.
- There is greater opportunity for increased income with less hours of work.

While there are benefits, one must look at the drawbacks:

- If people know co-workers in the group, they may act differently.

---

[14] Cockerham, Ginger. Group Coaching: A Comprehensive Blueprint. Bloomington, IN: IUniverse, 2011.

- Controlling the person who wants to do all the talking may be tricky.
- It takes additional work to form a group and longer lead time.
- There is greater skill required in facilitating a group using coaching skills.

I have read several studies on the size of coaching groups. Columbia University did a study and their conclusion on the perfect size is seven participants, give or take one. This size gives the necessary energy to the group while allowing a member to be absent.

PICKING YOUR GROUP COACHING TOPIC

The first step in group coaching is to pick your topic and do your research to ascertain if there is enough interest to form a group. My first group was around the subject of working with volunteers. My target audience was people who work in children's ministry. After 35 years of pastoring, I knew there was a need for these leaders to work together and improve their own ministry.

You can pick any topic you want. Who needs help? Where are there people struggling to reach their goals. The field is wide open and only limited by one's imagination.

You don't need to create the whole program until you have formed your group. I guarantee what you create before forming the group will need to be altered after forming your group and seeing the needs of the participants.

FORMING A GROUP

Ginger taught us well when she explained the importance of finding your advocates when forming your groups. Who believes in you and what you are doing so strongly that they will take your message to those they know? Your advocates know you, like you, and trust you to the degree that they are willing to recommend you and your work. Make a list of 10-12 advocates. Approach your advocates and ask them to help you help others.

POSSIBLE AGENDA

You might be asking the question, what will the group time look like? Great question! Many groups run for 90 minutes each session. The number of sessions depends on your goal and how you are structuring the group. Some groups run for a set number of sessions, while other groups are ongoing.

Before the session you may want to send out an email reminding the participants of the sessions and asking what they would like to add to the agenda. Remember, in coaching the coachee or client holds and sets the agenda.

Here is a sample agenda:

- Quick one minute check-in by all members
- Most successful achievement since last session
- Greatest challenge since last session
- Review submitted topics for discussion and allow group to set direction
- Proceed with the challenges presented and needing help
- Quick goal setting by all members
- How was this call valuable for you?
- What are you taking away?

LASER SPEAK

A key skill to teach in your group is "laser speak." People often want to go into great detail and long examples. In a group session there is limited time and many challenges to work on. Teaching laser speak at the beginning of the group time, and reminding the participants each session to use laser speak, is a necessary component of a group.

What is "laser speak?" When you share as one of the group participants, be quick and to the point. If other members of the group need more clarification, they will ask for it. As the coach, you will often need to remind some members of the group to use laser speak.

BRINGING A GROUP TO A CLOSE

When the group has completed the coaching program, it is important to look ahead to your next group. Here are some ideas to work on for the next group:

- What went right?
- What changes need to be considered?
- Who in this group are your new advocates?
- Who might want to join the next group?
- Is there a new group with a new topic that needs to be formed?

I personally enjoy group coaching and find the challenge to be energizing. In reality, I find the whole field of coaching to be pleasurable and an engaging occupation. I am encouraged when people find new awareness and make better choices because we have worked together. After reading this book I trust you will have new skills and a fresh desire to help others along this journey we call life.

Before we wrap up this tome, in the last chapter, I want to share with you the Top 10 Myths about coaching.

Dr. Bill Graybill

12

THE LAST WORD

As we wrap up this journey, I want to share with you an article by Robert Pagliarin. He covers the Top 10 Myths about life coaching by giving clear answers and bringing clarity to the subject. I present it to you as found on the CBS News site unedited.

TOP TEN PROFESSIONAL LIFE COACHING MYTHS

Life coaching is all the rage. Harvard Business Review reports that coaching is a $1 billion a year industry, but just what is a personal coach, professional coach, or life coach and why are so many executives and individuals using them to catapult their careers, break free from 9-5 jobs, and to create better, more fulfilling, richer lives?

First, what is a professional coach? The International Coach Federation (ICF) -- the leading global coaching organization and professional association for coaches -- defines coaching as "partnering with clients in a thought-provoking and creative process that inspires them to maximize their personal and professional potential."

Second, who's using coaches? In a 2009 study of the professional coaching industry by the Chartered Institute of Personnel Development (CIPD), they found that coaching was used by 90% of organizations surveyed and that even in the economic downturn, 70% report that they are increasing or maintaining their commitment to coaching. Coaching is clearly popular, but what does a professional coach do?

As with any growing profession, there can be a lot of confusion. To help distinguish fact from fiction, click (read) through the pages to read the top 10 personal coaching myths...

Myth 1: Life coaches are professionals who can help you achieve your goals.

Fact: Some, but certainly not all coaches are professionals who can help you reach your goals. One of the problems in the coaching industry is that anyone can call themselves a professional coach, life coach, personal coach, etc. Jennifer Corbin, the president of Coach U, one of the largest and oldest coach training organizations in the world, has said, "Technically, anyone can hang up a shingle as coaching is not regulated. Many people 'coaching' have no idea what coaching is as they haven't been trained or haven't been coached by a professionally trained and credentialed coach. There are 'schools' that will offer a credential after three hours of training and people read a book or watch a TV program and decide 'I'm a coach!'" As a result, the quality of coaches vary dramatically

Myth 2: Executive coaching is a nice employment perk.

Fact: Coaching is as much a perk to your employees as are their computers. Employees may view coaching as a value added benefit, but the successful organizations see coaching as something much more than a perk. Done right, professional coaching can drive sales, employee engagement, creativity, workplace satisfaction, and bottom line results. Wellness programs have been shown to provide approximately a 300% return on investment (ROI). In other words, companies who spend $1 in a wellness program (e.g., exercise clubs, personal trainers, smoking cessation workshops) earn $3 as a result of decreased turnover, fewer sick days, reduced health insurance costs, etc. It's no wonder wellness programs have experienced such tremendous growth -- it makes financial sense.

The ROI from professional coaching is even more astonishing. According to a Manchester Consulting Group study of Fortune 100 executives, the Economic Times reports "coaching resulted in a ROI of almost six times the program cost as well as a 77% improvement in relationships, 67% improvement in teamwork, 61% improvement in job satisfaction and 48% improvement in quality."

Myth 3: Personal coaches can only help you reach personal goals / Professional coaches can only help you reach business goals.

Fact: A good coach is someone who is an expert at helping others create positive change in their lives. For some clients, the positive change they most want may be focused on personal goals such as relationships, time management, work-life balance, stress reduction, simplification, health, etc., but other clients may be more interested in professional or business goals such as leadership, getting a promotion, starting a business, etc. An effective coach works with the client to help them live a better, richer life - regardless of their type of goals.

Myth 4: Professional coaching is for "problem" employees.

Fact: Coaching used to be a euphemism for "you're doing lousy work, but before we can fire you we need to show that we've done everything we can to support you so we don't get hit with an employment lawsuit." No more. According to Paul Michelman, editor of Harvard Business School's Management Update, "whereas coaching was once viewed by many as a tool to help correct underperformance, today it is becoming much more widely used in supporting top producers. Good coaching focuses on an individual's strengths and aims to help the client achieve what they want more of in life and at work. The goal? To help the client identify and achieve their greater goals and to help them live a better life. A good coach isn't there to "fix" anyone, but to help the client navigate toward a more engaged and compelling future.

Myth 5: Personal coaching takes too much time.

Fact: Professional coaching is a high-leverage activity. Clients can achieve remarkable progress toward their desired future in less than an hour per month of coaching. There is a wide spectrum of how coaching is delivered. Some coaches prefer to meet one-on-one with clients in an office, but most recommend telephone sessions for the ease of use, minimization of distractions, better privacy, greater efficiency, and for (yes, apparently) better connection to the client. Best practices in coaching call for between two and four sessions per month that last at least 20 minutes and up to 60 minutes. A sweet spot for many coaches and clients seems to be three sessions per month for 20 to 45 minutes a session - a miniscule investment of time for the results achieved.

Myth 6: Life coaches are like having a good friend to bounce ideas off and to keep you motivated.

Fact: Your coach may be friendly, but they are not your friend. Your coach is your advocate. They want the best from you. They will work with you to help you reach your goals and to succeed. Your coach will hold you accountable and challenge you to grow and do more than you think you can do. They may push, pull, and stretch you in ways that may feel uncomfortable. And unlike a friendship, the coaching relationship is unilateral - it is exclusively focused on you and your goals, not the coach, his family, his golf handicap, or what she did over the weekend.

Myth 7: Executive coaching is only good for upper management / Coaching is only good for entry level employees.

Fact: Coaching is good for anyone who is motivated to create a better life. Initially professional coaching or executive coaching was for upper management, and some organizations still focus their coaching efforts on their top performers. Now, more and more companies are recognizing the powerful benefits of providing coaching to rank and file employees. For example, online shoe and clothing company Zappos.com, known for their outstanding commitment to creating a culture of unparalleled customer service (they even teach this through Zappos Insights), has a full-time goals coach who works with any employee - not just management - on helping them create better lives.

Myth 8: Professional coaches tell their clients what to do and give them advice.

Fact: Bad or inexperienced coaches tell their clients what to do and are constantly giving advice. Good coaches do not. Most clients realize they don't need another parent, sibling, friend, or co-worker telling you what you should be doing. Instead, coaches help their clients explore and come up with the best choices for them based on where they are and the client's vision for their future. Coaches are experts at the process of changing behavior, which is much more valuable than giving instructions.

Myth 9: Executive coaching is expensive.

Fact: Coaching can cost a great deal of money. Harvard Business School's "What can Coaches do for You?" research whitepaper reports some executive coaches cost up to $3,500 for an hour of coaching. While this is an extreme, most personal coaches charge a monthly retainer between $500 to $2,000 a month. What this means is that either there are a lot of really stupid people wasting their money on coaching each month or they are getting results worth at least the cost of their coach. According to the ICF Global Coaching Client Study commissioned by the International Coach Federation, individual clients reported a median ROI of 3.44 times their investment in coaching. Bottom line, coaching is an investment that can produce monetary rewards above and beyond the cost.

Myth 10: Professional coaching is spiritual and relies on "harnessing the energy in the universe."

Fact: I have no idea what "harnessing the power of the universe" means, and my guess is that most professional coaches don't either. When I first started researching coaching, I was under the impression coaching involved lots of chanting, incense, meditation, and other spiritual practices. While there are many great spiritual coaches that may incorporate these practices into their session, most coaches are practical, professional, business people who are focused on tangible results, not airy-fairy mysticism. You can leave your granola and Birkenstocks at home.[15]

Robert Pagliarini is obsessed with inspiring others to create and empowering them to live life to the fullest by radically changing the way they invest their time and energy. He is the founder of Richer Life, a community of passionate people who want to learn and achieve more in life and at work. He is a Certified Financial Planner and the president of Pacifica Wealth Advisors, a boutique wealth management firm serving sudden wealth recipients and affluent individuals. He has appeared as a financial expert on 20/20, Good Morning America, Dr. Phil, Dr. Drew's Lifechangers and many others.

---

[15] REPRINTED WITH PERMISSION of the author. Slight editing for space. http://www.cbsnews.com/news/top-10-professional-life-coaching-myths/10/

Dr. Bill Graybill

The Wheel of Life

When using the Wheel of Life, I have the coachee evaluate each area of their life on the wheel. Under each area blacken in the section that represents how that area scores. This produces a visual picture of their life. It reveals what areas are needing work and why life might be very bumpy.

I have them choose the top three areas they want to work on. Under each area I have them list three reasons why that area is important. Depending on the coachee, I may ask for three steps they could take instead of the reason why it is important.

Use your imagination when working with this tool. It can open the door to many different aspects of life coaching.

I use a similar exercise for ministry coaching. I simply change the areas to the following areas:

- Volunteer Recruitment
- Volunteer Training/Care
- Volunteer Resourcing
- Your Leadership Development
- Outreach
- Facilities
- Spiritual and Prayer Life
- Organization
- Special Events
- Teamwork

WHEEL OF LIFE

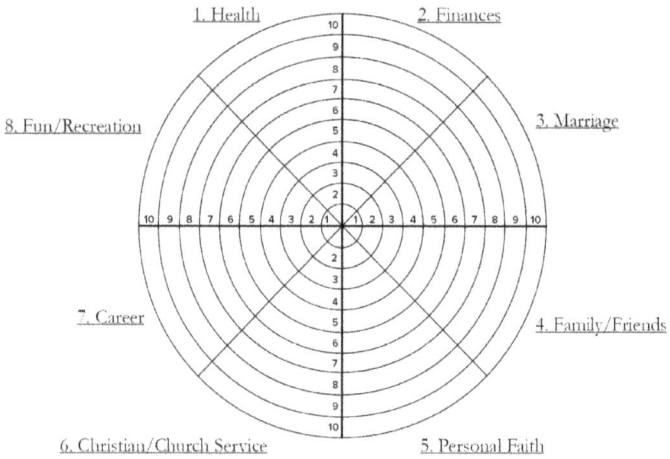

1. Health
2. Finances
8. Fun/Recreation
3. Marriage
7. Career
4. Family/Friends
6. Christian/Church Service
5. Personal Faith

1. _____

    A. _____

    B. _____

    C. _____

2. _____

    A. _____

    B. _____

    C. _____

3. _____

    A. _____

    B. _____

    C. _____

APPENDIX B

Values Inventory

From the following list, circle the words that best describe what is important to you, that cause you to feel passion. Try to limit it to 20 words. These words are in no special order.

Tolerance	Freedom	Relationship	Financial
Honesty	Exploration	Team	Independence
Genuineness	Creativity	Community	Stewardship
Authenticity	Fun	Belonging	Frugality
Accountability	Artistic	Depth	Overflow
Integrity	Spontaneity	Being known	Sharing
Directness	Flexibility	Intimacy	Benevolence
Sincerity	Knowledge	Commitment	Justice
Strength	The search	Friendship	Life-long learning
Character	Meaning	Communication	Investment
Follow-through	Influence	Gentleness	Success
Sacrifice	Truth	Compassion	Recognition
Legacy	Passion	Caring	Community action
Family Marriage	Seeing the world	Emotion	Career advancement
Duty	Adventure	Self-gratification	Efficiency
Honor	Diversity	Health	Accomplishment
Heritage	Travel	Devotion	Focus
Responsibility	Change	Passionate pursuit	Purpose
Harmony	Movement	Worship	Achievement
Security	New Challenges	Generosity	Building
Stability	Opportunity	Service	Leadership
Peace	Enthusiasm	Reflection	Mastery
Home	Starting things	Reaching out	Competence
Thoughtfulness	Entrepreneurial	Evangelism	Precision
Practicality	Motivation	Changing the world	Excellence
Nurture	Progress	Hospitality	Planning
Love	Inspiration	Concern	Being knowledgeable
Beauty	Renewal	Making a difference	Principles
Romance	Healing	Social justice	Rationality
Volunteering	Nature	Reliability	Spiritual integrity
Disciplining	Empowering others	Positive impact	Encouraging
Ambition	Enlightenment	Growth	Respect for life
Being in control	Faithfulness	Humor	Risk taking
Caution	Forgiveness	Orderliness	Self-expression
Collaboration	Forward-looking	Persistence	Servanthood
Competition	Collecting	Personal power	Respect for
Determination	Winning	Respect for people	environment
Diligence	Trust	Hard work	Solitude
Purity	Tolerance	Independence	Spiritual growth
Independence	Mentoring	Obedience	Self-esteem
Joy	Sensitivity	Humility	Relaxation

Copyright © 2009 Bill Graybill Coaching, LLC. All Rights Reserved

Values Inventory

Current Values
List the top five values that have consistently been present in your life over the past six months.

1.
2.
3.
4.
5.

List your current values in order of priority.

1.
2.
3.
4.
5.

List your ideal values in order of priority.

1.
2.
3.
4.
5.

ICF Core Competencies

The following eleven core coaching competencies were developed to support greater understanding about the skills and approaches used within today's coaching profession as defined by the International Coach Federation. They will also support you in calibrating the level of alignment between the coach-specific training expected and the training you have experienced.

Finally, these competencies and the ICF definition were used as the foundation for the ICF Credentialing process examination. The ICF defines coaching as partnering with clients in a thought-provoking and creative process that inspires them to maximize their personal and professional potential. The Core Competencies are grouped into four clusters according to those that fit together logically based on common ways of looking at the competencies in each group. The groupings and individual competencies are not weighted—they do not represent any kind of priority in that they are all core or critical for any competent coach to demonstrate.

A. Setting the Foundation
1. Meeting Ethical Guidelines and Professional Standards
2. Establishing the Coaching Agreement

B. Co-creating the Relationship
3. Establishing Trust and Intimacy with the Client
4. Coaching Presence

C. Communicating Effectively
5. Active Listening

6. Powerful Questioning
7. Direct Communication

D. Facilitating Learning and Results
8. Creating Awareness
9. Designing Actions
10. Planning and Goal Setting
11. Managing Progress and Accountability

A. SETTING THE FOUNDATION

1. Meeting Ethical Guidelines and Professional Standards—
Understanding of coaching ethics and standards and ability to
apply them appropriately in all coaching situations.

1. Understands and exhibits in own behaviors the ICF
   Standards of Conduct (see list, Part III of ICF Code of
   Ethics).
2. Understands and follows all ICF Ethical Guidelines (see
   list).
3. Clearly communicates the distinctions between
   coaching, consulting, psychotherapy and other support
   professions.
4. Refers client to another support professional as needed,
   knowing when this is needed and the available
   resources.

2. Establishing the Coaching Agreement—Ability to understand
what is required in the specific coaching interaction and to come
to agreement with the prospective and new client about the
coaching process and relationship.

1. Understands and effectively discusses with the client the
   guidelines and specific parameters of the coaching
   relationship (e.g., logistics, fees, scheduling, inclusion of
   others if appropriate).

2. Reaches agreement about what is appropriate in the relationship and what is not, what is and is not being offered, and about the client's and coach's responsibilities.

3. Determines whether there is an effective match between his/her coaching method and the needs of the prospective client.

B. CO-CREATING THE RELATIONSHIP

3. Establishing Trust and Intimacy with the Client—Ability to create a safe, supportive environment that produces ongoing mutual respect and trust.

1. Shows genuine concern for the client's welfare and future.
2. Continuously demonstrates personal integrity, honesty and sincerity.
3. Establishes clear agreements and keeps promises.
4. Demonstrates respect for client's perceptions, learning style, personal being.
5. Provides ongoing support for and champions new behaviors and actions, including those involving risk taking and fear of failure.
6. Asks permission to coach client in sensitive, new areas.

4. Coaching Presence—Ability to be fully conscious and create spontaneous relationship with the client, employing a style that is open, flexible and confident.

1. Is present and flexible during the coaching process, dancing in the moment.
2. Accesses own intuition and trusts one's inner knowing—"goes with the gut."
3. Is open to not knowing and takes risks.
4. Sees many ways to work with the client and chooses in the moment what is most effective.

5. Uses humor effectively to create lightness and energy.
6. Confidently shifts perspectives and experiments with new possibilities for own action.
7. Demonstrates confidence in working with strong emotions and can self-manage and not be overpowered or enmeshed by client's emotions.

C. COMMUNICATING EFFECTIVELY

5. Active Listening—Ability to focus completely on what the client is saying and is not saying, to understand the meaning of what is said in the context of the client's desires, and to support client self-expression.

1. Attends to the client and the client's agenda and not to the coach's agenda for the client.
2. Hears the client's concerns, goals, values and beliefs about what is and is not possible.
3. Distinguishes between the words, the tone of voice, and the body language.
4. Summarizes, paraphrases, reiterates, and mirrors back what client has said to ensure clarity and understanding.
5. Encourages, accepts, explores and reinforces the client's expression of feelings, perceptions, concerns, beliefs, suggestions, etc.
6. Integrates and builds on client's ideas and suggestions.
7. "Bottom-lines" or understands the essence of the client's communication and helps the client get there rather than engaging in long, descriptive stories.
8. Allows the client to vent or "clear" the situation without judgment or attachment in order to move on to next steps.

6. Powerful Questioning—Ability to ask questions that reveal the information needed for maximum benefit to the coaching relationship and the client.

1. Asks questions that reflect active listening and an understanding of the client's perspective.
2. Asks questions that evoke discovery, insight, commitment or action (e.g., those that challenge the client's assumptions).
3. Asks open-ended questions that create greater clarity, possibility or new learning.
4. Asks questions that move the client toward what they desire, not questions that ask for the client to justify or look backward.

7. Direct Communication—Ability to communicate effectively during coaching sessions, and to use language that has the greatest positive impact on the client.

1. Is clear, articulate and direct in sharing and providing feedback.
2. Reframes and articulates to help the client understand from another perspective what he/she wants or is uncertain about.
3. Clearly states coaching objectives, meeting agenda, and purpose of techniques or exercises.
4. Uses language appropriate and respectful to the client (e.g., non-sexist, non-racist, non-technical, non-jargon).
5. Uses metaphor and analogy to help to illustrate a point or paint a verbal picture.

D. FACILITATING LEARNING AND RESULTS

8. Creating Awareness—Ability to integrate and accurately evaluate multiple sources of information and to make interpretations that help the client to gain awareness and thereby achieve agreed-upon results.

1. Goes beyond what is said in assessing client's concerns, not getting hooked by the client's description.
2. Invokes inquiry for greater understanding, awareness,

and clarity.

3. Identifies for the client his/her underlying concerns; typical and fixed ways of perceiving himself/herself and the world; differences between the facts and the interpretation; and disparities between thoughts, feelings, and action.

4. Helps clients to discover for themselves the new thoughts, beliefs, perceptions, emotions, moods, etc. that strengthen their ability to take action and achieve what is important to them.

5. Communicates broader perspectives to clients and inspires commitment to shift their viewpoints and find new possibilities for action.

6. Helps clients to see the different, interrelated factors that affect them and their behaviors (e.g., thoughts, emotions, body, and background).

7. Expresses insights to clients in ways that are useful and meaningful for the client.

8. Identifies major strengths vs. major areas for learning and growth, and what is most important to address during coaching.

9. Asks the client to distinguish between trivial and significant issues, situational vs. recurring behaviors, when detecting a separation between what is being stated and what is being done.

9. Designing Actions—Ability to create with the client opportunities for ongoing learning, during coaching and in work/life situations, and for taking new actions that will most effectively lead to agreed-upon coaching results.

1. Brainstorms and assists the client to define actions that will enable the client to demonstrate, practice, and deepen new learning.

2. Helps the client to focus on and systematically explore specific concerns and opportunities that are central to agreed-upon coaching goals.

3. Engages the client to explore alternative ideas and solutions, to evaluate options, and to make related decisions.
4. Promotes active experimentation and self-discovery, where the client applies what has been discussed and learned during sessions immediately afterward in his/her work or life setting.
5. Celebrates client successes and capabilities for future growth.
6. Challenges client's assumptions and perspectives to provoke new ideas and find new possibilities for action.
7. Advocates or brings forward points of view that are aligned with client goals and, without attachment, engages the client to consider them.
8. Helps the client "Do It Now" during the coaching session, providing immediate support.
9. Encourages stretches and challenges but also a comfortable pace of learning.

10. Planning and Goal Setting—Ability to develop and maintain an effective coaching plan with the client.

1. Consolidates collected information and establishes a coaching plan and development goals with the client that address concerns and major areas for learning and development.
2. Creates a plan with results that are attainable, measurable, specific, and have target dates.
3. Makes plan adjustments as warranted by the coaching process and by changes in the situation.
4. Helps the client identify and access different resources for learning (e.g., books, other professionals).
5. Identifies and targets early successes that are important to the client.

11. Managing Progress and Accountability—Ability to hold attention on what is important for the client, and to leave responsibility with the client to take action.

1. Clearly requests of the client actions that will move the client toward his/her stated goals.
2. Demonstrates follow-through by asking the client about those actions that the client committed to during the previous session(s).
3. Acknowledges the client for what they have done, not done, learned or become aware of since the previous coaching session(s).
4. Effectively prepares, organizes, and reviews with client information obtained during sessions.
5. Keeps the client on track between sessions by holding attention on the coaching plan and outcomes, agreed-upon courses of action, and topics for future session(s).
6. Focuses on the coaching plan but is also open to adjusting behaviors and actions based on the coaching process and shifts in direction during sessions.
7. Is able to move back and forth between the big picture of where the client is heading, setting a context for what is being discussed and where the client wishes to go.
8. Promotes client's self-discipline and holds the client accountable for what they say they are going to do, for the results of an intended action, or for a specific plan with related time frames.
9. Develops the client's ability to make decisions, address key concerns, and develop himself/herself (to get feedback, to determine priorities and set the pace of learning, to reflect on and learn from experiences).
10. Positively confronts the client with the fact that he/she did not take agreed-upon actions.[16]

---

[16] International Coach Federation, "Core Competencies," coachfederation.org, accessed April 7, 2015, http://www.coachfederation.org/credential/landing.cfm?ItemNumber=2206&navItemNumber=576. Unedited

APPENDIX D

ICF Code of Ethics

PART ONE: DEFINITION OF COACHING

Section 1: Definitions

- Coaching: Coaching is partnering with clients in a thought-provoking and creative process that inspires them to maximize their personal and professional potential
- A professional coaching relationship: A professional coaching relationship exists when coaching includes a business agreement or contract that defines the responsibilities of each party.
- An ICF Professional Coach: An ICF Professional Coach also agrees to practice the ICF Professional Core Competencies and pledges accountability to the ICF Code of Ethics.

In order to clarify roles in the coaching relationship, it is often necessary to distinguish between the client and the sponsor. In most cases, the client and sponsor are the same person and therefore jointly referred to as the client. For purposes of identification, however, the International Coach Federation defines these roles as follows:

- Client: The "client" is the person(s) being coached.
- Sponsor: The "sponsor" is the entity (including its representatives) paying for and/or arranging for coaching services to be provided.

In all cases, coaching engagement contracts or agreements should clearly establish the rights, roles, and responsibilities for both the client and sponsor if they are not the same persons.

PART TWO: THE ICF STANDARDS OF ETHICAL
CONDUCT

Preamble: ICF Professional Coaches aspire to conduct
themselves in a manner that reflects positively upon the
coaching profession; are respectful of different approaches to
coaching; and recognize that they are also bound by applicable
laws and regulations.

Section 1: Professional Conduct At Large

As a coach:

1) I will not knowingly make any public statement that is untrue
or misleading about what I offer as a coach or make false claims
in any written documents relating to the coaching profession or
my credentials or the ICF.

2) I will accurately identify my coaching qualifications, expertise,
experience, certifications and ICF Credentials.

3) I will recognize and honor the efforts and contributions of
others and not misrepresent them as my own. I understand that
violating this standard may leave me subject to legal remedy by a
third party.

4) I will, at all times, strive to recognize personal issues that may
impair, conflict or interfere with my coaching performance or
my professional coaching relationships. Whenever the facts and
circumstances necessitate, I will promptly seek professional
assistance and determine the action to be taken, including
whether it is appropriate to suspend or terminate my coaching
relationship(s).

5) I will conduct myself in accordance with the ICF Code of Ethics in all coach training, coach mentoring and coach supervisory activities.

6) I will conduct and report research with competence, honesty and within recognized scientific standards and applicable subject guidelines. My research will be carried out with the necessary consent and approval of those involved and with an approach that will protect participants from any potential harm. All research efforts will be performed in a manner that complies with all the applicable laws of the country in which the research is conducted.

7) I will maintain, store, and dispose of any records created during my coaching business in a manner that promotes confidentiality, security and privacy, and complies with any applicable laws and agreements

8) I will use ICF Member contact information (email addresses, telephone numbers, etc.) only in the manner and to the extent authorized by the ICF.

Section 2: Conflicts of Interest

As a coach:

9) I will seek to avoid conflicts of interest and potential conflicts of interest and openly disclose any such conflicts. I will offer to remove myself when such a conflict arises.

10) I will disclose to my client and his or her sponsor all anticipated compensation from third parties that I may pay or receive for referrals of that client.

11) I will only barter for services, goods or other non-monetary remuneration when it will not impair the coaching relationship.

12) I will not knowingly take any personal, professional or monetary advantage or benefit of the coach-client relationship, except by a form of compensation as agreed in the agreement or contract.

Section 3: Professional Conduct with Clients

As a coach:

13) I will not knowingly mislead or make false claims about what my client or sponsor will receive from the coaching process or from me as the coach.

14) I will not give my prospective clients or sponsors information or advice I know or believe to be misleading or false.

15) I will have clear agreements or contracts with my clients and sponsor(s). I will honor all agreements or contracts made in the context of professional coaching relationships.

16) I will carefully explain and strive to ensure that, prior to or at the initial meeting, my coaching client and sponsor(s) understand the nature of coaching, the nature and limits of confidentiality, financial arrangements, and any other terms of the coaching agreement or contract.

17) I will be responsible for setting clear, appropriate, and culturally sensitive boundaries that govern any physical contact I may have with my clients or sponsors.

18) I will not become sexually intimate with any of my current clients or sponsors.

19) I will respect the client's right to terminate the coaching relationship at any point during the process, subject to the

provisions of the agreement or contract. I will be alert to indications that the client is no longer benefiting from our coaching relationship.

20) I will encourage the client or sponsor to make a change if I believe the client or sponsor would be better served by another coach or by another resource.

21) I will suggest my client seek the services of other professionals when deemed necessary or appropriate.

Section 4: Confidentiality/Privacy

As a coach:

22) I will maintain the strictest levels of confidentiality with all client and sponsor information. I will have a clear agreement or contract before releasing information to another person, unless required by law.

23) I will have a clear agreement upon how coaching information will be exchanged among coach, client and sponsor.

24) When acting as a trainer of student coaches, I will clarify confidentiality policies with the students.

25) I will have associated coaches and other persons whom I manage in service of my clients and their sponsors in a paid or volunteer capacity make clear agreements or contracts to adhere to the ICF Code of Ethics Part 2, Section 4: Confidentiality/Privacy standards and the entire ICF Code of Ethics to the extent applicable.

PART THREE: THE ICF PLEDGE OF ETHICS

As an ICF Professional Coach, I acknowledge and agree to honor my ethical and legal obligations to my coaching clients and sponsors, colleagues, and to the public at large. I pledge to comply with the ICF Code of Ethics and to practice these standards with those whom I coach.

If I breach this Pledge of Ethics or any part of the ICF Code of Ethics, I agree that the ICF in its sole discretion may hold me accountable for so doing. I further agree that my accountability to the ICF for any breach may include sanctions, such as loss of my ICF Membership and/or my ICF Credentials.

Approved by the Ethics and Standards Committee on October 30, 2008.

Approved by the ICF Board of Directors on December 18, 2008.[17]

---

[17] International Coach Federation, "Code of Ethics," coachfederation.org, accessed April 7, 2015, http://coachfederation.org/about/ethics.aspx?ItemNumber=854&_ga=1.1124619 56.1687759353.1423186325&RDtoken=43942&userID=13417. Unedited

ABOUT THE AUTHOR

Bill Graybill, D.Min., PCC, is an executive coach, trainer, speaker, adjunct professor, former pastor and best-selling author. His focus is on conflict resolution, anger management and organizational health. He currently serves as president of Peace Mentors, a non-profit organization dedicated to Redemptive Conflict Resolution.™

Congregations and groups of all types enjoy and appreciate his presentations, filled with solid biblical understanding and practical application, delivered with humor. Bill connects quickly with audiences and invites them to join him on a journey of resolving their conflicts God's way.

Bill coaches individuals and teams in businesses and non-profit organizations. Having pastored Abundant Life Center for 35 years, and over 40 years of professional experience, he brings understanding, a broad-base skill set, and passion to those he serves.

As an Adjunct Faculty Member of Western Seminary, Global University and Kenya College of Ministry, Bill teaches conflict management cross-culturally from local trainings to graduate level.

Bill and his wife, Dorothy, live in Albany, Oregon, with Buddy their golden retriever. They have two married sons, Dan and Mark, and four grandkids.

OTHER RESOURCES

Resolve Conflict God's Way; The Skills You Need to Make Peace An Amazon Best Seller.

Resolve Conflict God's Way provides step-by-step guidance to redemptive conflict resolution and mending broken relationships. Through biblical principles and practical worksheets, you will learn new strategies to resolve conflict.

If you are in the middle of conflict, you can make immediate changes by learning:

1. When it is okay to get angry and when it is not okay.
2. How to manage your anger so you do not destroy those you love.
3. How to walk in true forgiveness even when the pain is great.
4. How to deal with difficult people with God's love.
5. The ABC's of confessing your sin so others will forgive you.
6. How to heal relationships by confronting others.

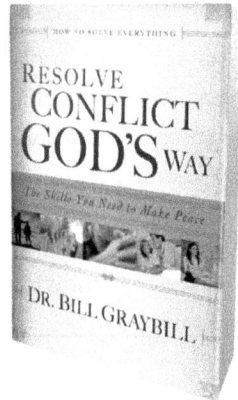

Bonus material is available at the end of each chapter to further your journey into Redemptive Conflict Resolution.™

Order your copy from resolveconflictgodsway.com or other online bookstores.

Endorsed by Dr. Eugene Peterson, Rick Warren's Newsletter and Pastors.com.

Available in English, Spanish and Kindle formats.

OTHER RESOURCES

Coaching Conflict for Healthy Outcomes; A Complete Conflict Coaching Course

Here is your chance to learn the secrets of coaching conflict. In a world of high tension and increasing conflict, it is vitally important to have the coaching skills to bring peace to individuals and organizations.

This course is based on the book: Resolve Conflict God's Way; The Skills You Need to Make Peace. It is 16 hours in length and is accepted by the ICF for credits towards certification. This course is taught live on site, and through webinars.

"Recently I attended Bill's Coaching Conflict for Healthy Outcomes 2-day class. I found the content Bill provided in this course to far exceed the cost of the class and the time and expense of traveling out of state to attend. I see many applications in my own life, as well as in the lives of those who come to me for Leadership Coaching. Bill's class has given me several new tools to use in my practice. I look forward to following in his footsteps as a peace mentor."

Greg Cottrill, CTC, ACC,
Leadership Coach @ Go Forth Coaching

For more information on this course contact Bill Graybill at bill@peacementors.com

Newsletter and other resources are available at www.PeaceMentors.com.

ABOUT PEACE MENTORS

VISION STATEMENT
Peace Mentors is a partner to Christian leaders creating positive environments and redemptive conflict solutions.

MISSION STATEMENT
Peace Mentors works with leaders and leadership teams to build cultures where people thrive and experience greater success. Through quality education, effective leadership training, intentional strategic planning and redemptive conflict management, organizations experience a high degree of influence.

CORE VALUES
Integrity is the foundation of all relationships.
Relationships give us the greatest joy and purpose in this life.
Encouragement gives vibrancy to a relationship.
Reliability builds trust, confidence, and integrity.
Empowering others creates my greatest success.
A Positive Impact is my contribution to society.

WHAT PEACE MENTORS OFFERS
- Executive coaching
- Team and organizational coaching
- Conflict resolution in teams and organizations
- Sunday congregational ministry
- Church seminars and workshops
- Resources

For more information go to PeaceMentors.com or contact me by phone or email.
Phone: 541-791-6544
Email: bill@peacementors.com

Dr. Bill Graybill

www.ingramcontent.com/pod-product-compliance
Lightning Source LLC
Chambersburg PA
CBHW060615210326
41520CB00010B/1351